Z, 3-

STEPHANIE WINSTON'S
BEST ORGANIZING TIPS

Quick, simple ways

to get organized

and get on with your life

STEPHANIE WINSTON

A FIRESIDE BOOK
PUBLISHED BY SIMON & SCHUSTER
New York London Toronto
Sydney Tokyo Singapore

FIRESIDE
Rockefeller Center
1230 Avenue of the Americas
New York, NY 10020

First Fireside Edition 1996

FIRESIDE and colophon are registered trademarks
of Simon & Schuster Inc.

Designed by Pei Loi Koay

Manufactured in the United States of America

1   3   5   7   9   10   8   6   4   2

3   5   7   9   10   8   6   4   Pbk.

Library of Congress Cataloging-in-Publication Data
Winston, Stephanie.
Stephanie Winston's best organizing tips : quick, simple ways to get
organized and get on with your life / Stephanie Winston.
p.   cm.
Includes bibliographical references and index.
1. Time management.   2. Organization.   3. Home economics.
I. Title.   II. Title: Best organizing tips.
HD69.T54W55   1995
640'.43—dc20   94-27012
CIP
ISBN: 0-671-88643-6
ISBN: 0-684-81824-8 Pbk.

Acknowledgments

Many thanks to the wonderful professionals who helped so much with the development of this project: to my editor, Fred Hills, who was the first to see the need for this book, and whose encouragement, support, and energy brought it to fruition; to Marnie Winston-Macauley, wordsmith extraordinaire, whose ability to come up with just the right way to organize and frame the material in this book was unerring and uncanny; to Laureen Connelly Rowland, whose thorough and thoroughly excellent line editing put the final polish on this book; and to my agent, Jay Acton, for his unfailing support and belief that it would all come right in the end.

to my family and dear friends

Contents

STEPHANIE WINSTON'S
BEST ORGANIZING TIPS

How to Use This Book

Do you ever feel that if your children, spouse, or boss demand one more thing from you, you're going to explode? If so, take comfort in the fact that you are not alone. For more than a decade, unprecedented numbers of Americans have been suffering from too many things to do and too little time to do them. If you are one of the overstressed and overworked, you've no doubt heard yourself say, "If only there were twenty-seven hours in the day," "If only I could clear my desk," "If only my clothes didn't bury me every time I open my closet," "If only I could get rid of clutter," "If only I could find some time for myself."

Most of us do get overwhelmed by our conflicting priorities, so very often, we (literally) push aside things that don't *seem* so important—like yesterday's junk mail or tomorrow's agenda. But there is a way to get through today *and* be prepared for tomorrow, if you consider your problems as an exciting opportunity to get organized and get on with your life!

Perhaps your current state of disorganization has diminished your productivity at the office . . . perhaps you always find yourself arriving red-faced, breathless—and ten minutes late . . . or perhaps your palms get sweaty at the very thought of getting organized. Regardless of the reason—fear not, *it can be done!* Your organizational problems can be solved and your life will become more livable with the help of some very basic, easy-to-implement time- and space-saving tips.

The idea for a handy guide of best tips was born after my first book, *Getting Organized,* was published. That book introduced the basic principles of getting organized, but I soon began getting letters from readers asking "Isn't there one handy book in which I can find all the organizing answers I need at my fingertips?"

So here it is: a cornucopia of straight solutions, garnered from my own experience and from the wealth of knowledge of other experts in the field. Each tip is a sixty-second problem solver designed to help you figure out what to do when, and how to create a physical environment that is easy to move around in, easy to look at, and easy to function in. You'll soon discover that clearing the clutter—on your desk, in your kitchen, closet, or garage—will enhance your productivity at work and at home.

For your convenience, *Stephanie Winston's Best Organizing Tips* is divided into four parts: paper, time, closets and clutter, and home management. Each of the eighteen topical chapters addresses common organizational problems and offers on-the-spot explanations for how to solve them. If, for example, you're wondering how to organize your children's toys, look up "toys" in the index and you'll find the answer in Part Four.

Since desk mess is often found at the core of disorganization and is the easiest "symptom" to identify, I have decided to start with paper tips. Many of my clients find that freeing up their desk (which is often the toughest hurdle) inspires them to tackle other organizational hot spots they had long since given up on.

You will find some tips in more than one section. This is partly because not all of you are disorganized in the same way —someone with an organized closet probably won't need to work through the closet chapter, but might benefit from a similar tip in organizing her desk. Also, many of the tips are so organizationally sound they can practically be applied universally.

So, congratulations! You are on your way to organizing a life that "works"—a life of expansiveness, success, and peace of mind.

Good luck and good organizing!

Stephanie Winston

P.S. Please send in your own great organizing and time-management tips for a possible follow-up book. At the back of this book you'll find a page on which you can jot down your tips and any other comments you might have. I will personally review every suggestion that you are kind enough to send.

"Where Do I Start?"
An Organizing Inventory

How often have you cried "Help! My life's a mess!" It doesn't take much to feel overwhelmed by disarray, but believe it or not, even the biggest mess becomes manageable when it's broken down into specific problem areas. So instead of trying to tackle everything at once, first identify your individual organizational hot spots—those areas in your life you need to get control of now—by doing the following inventory:

First, check off each box on the left that applies to you. Then, in the box on the right, rank each of your problems on a scale of 1 to 5 by degree of annoyance or inconvenience—a #1 is for something mildly annoying, while a #5 drives you up the wall.

Once you have completed the inventory, take a long look at your #5's and #4's—believe it or not, it *is* possible to master even those tasks that seem to get the best of you. Select your first #5 and check the chapter headings and index for your areas of interest. Then get going! Next, turn to your next #5, and the one after that, and then the #4's. Work on down the priority list—and get on with your life!

The Paper Trap

☐ The clutter on my desk is compounding daily, and I don't know where to start.   ☐

☐ I'm afraid to file important papers because I fear I'll never find them again. But with everything "important" on my desk, I can't find *anything*.   ☐

☐ We've got magazines, newspapers, and catalogs on the dining room table, on the coffee table, and on our nightstands. Even if I wanted to read one, I'd never find it.   ☐

☐ I'm getting too many second notices (and nasty phone calls) because I just can't find my bills.   ☐

☐ Tax time is Tums time. Just the thought of getting everything together makes my stomach churn.   ☐

Get Time on Your Side!

☐ My friends and coworkers tease me 'cause I never call them back. I always *mean* to, but somehow it slips my mind.   ☐

☐ I'm so overwhelmed by "priorities" that between my job and family, I can't figure out what to do for whom first.   ☐

☐ I never get anything done and I never have time for myself. Wherever I turn I'm interrupted.   ☐

☐ I can't stop procrastinating. My proposals are always a day late, and I've been working with my Boy Scout troop on a project since they were Cub Scouts.   ☐

Clutter, Closets, and Home

☐ My household clutter seems to double daily. I just keep tripping over more stuff. ☐

☐ I'm tired of being bombarded by an avalanche of clothes and hangers every time I open the door. ☐

☐ The rooms in my home don't work—there's too much space where I don't need it, too little space where I want it, and I don't know how to make the most of the space I do have. ☐

☐ I've even tried bribing my kids to get them to pitch in with household chores. I'm afraid it's a lost cause. ☐

☐ My kids have such a hard time finding anything in their rooms that getting them out on time in the morning is next to impossible. ☐

☐ By the end of the day, I swear I've jogged a mile in my kitchen. I'd rather do that in the park. I'd give anything to have an organized, user-friendly kitchen. ☐

☐ I hate laundry. I hate cleaning. I hate chores. I've got to find ways to streamline these "must do's." ☐

THE
PAPER
TRAP

What to do with paper,

how to file it,

when to throw it away

1

Conquering
Paperwork Gridlock

Pat is a stringer for her local newspaper and can write authoritatively about anything from Thanksgiving chestnut stuffing to theater reviews. She also manages to make her deadlines. However, Pat has yet to file her health insurance claim from six months ago. Her desk is covered with story ideas and research for articles, unanswered letters, unpaid bills, and other hard-to-identify papers. And to the side of her desk is a large stack of unread magazines and newspapers, probably dating back six months.

Pat is caught in the paper trap.

Paper is perhaps *the* bane of our organizational existence, because paper is ubiquitous. Every day we are bombarded with, surrounded by, and submerged in an ever-increasing influx of printed material, from important things like the estimate on your gutter replacement to coupon Val-U-Paks. And every day we all do *something* with this paper—even if, like Pat, we only push it aside and say, in what I call the "Scarlett O'Hara syndrome," "I'll think about it tomorrow." But we seldom do. When this happens, the problem of paper becomes not a problem of neatness, but a problem of decision making.

If you are also prone to "push it aside," ask yourself this question whenever you come across a bill, catalog, bank statement, or coupon book: "What's the worst thing that could happen if this didn't exist?" If nothing would happen, *toss* it. If you think you might need it someday, can you find a duplicate if someday comes? If so, get rid of it.

Regardless of your response, a decision must be made, and the good news is there are only four possibilities:

T   *Toss.* As we've seen, you *can* throw it away.

R   *Refer.* It ain't your job, it's somebody else's. Pass it along to someone who might be interested in it or who is responsible for it.

A   *Act.* No getting around it, it *is* your job. Act on it personally: Reply to that letter, examine that report, sign that expense voucher.

F   *File.* Your only job is to find a place for it so you can find it again. Name it and file it.

I call this the TRAF system, and it is the fundamental rule of paperwork. Stick with this formula for decision making, and the wealth of handy TRAF tips in this section, and you can be sure you won't be tripped up or trapped by paper again.

TRAFing Your Way out of the Paper Trap

	CATEGORY	RECEPTACLE
TOSS	Might this paper have value for you now or in the future? If not, discard.	Wastebasket or recycling bin
REFER	Pass papers on to your secretary or staffers when they can handle them, or send to a colleague in whose area the matter falls.	Referral folders Out box
ACT	Act on any paper requiring a response from you—letter, analysis, review, etc.	Action box Reading stack
FILE	If a paper might have future value for you, file it. When possible, mark a discard date on it.	File box (your desk files) Out box (office files)

For starters—highlight

- Read mail with a highlighter or pen in hand. Mark or highlight any actions required—due dates on bills, expiration dates, appointments, invitation dates—and put the items in your action box.
- If you are setting aside a paper to keep—for example, an article you want to save—highlight the section that interests you so you won't have to read it all over again.

The TRAF System:
Toss, Refer, Act, and File

TOSS: Getting Rid of It

- Open your mail over the wastebasket, tossing as you go. In an apartment house, sort mail in the mailroom, bringing upstairs only materials you will be acting on. This reduces the paper load both literally and psychologically.
- For those papers you are unsure about: time to bite the bullet. For each piece of paper ask yourself, "What's the worst thing that could happen if it didn't exist?" If the answer is "nothing," *toss*. It your answer is, "Maybe I'll need it someday," ask yourself, "Can I find a duplicate if someday comes?" If so, get rid of it.
- Set up a "holding pen"—a special drawer—for papers you think you might need but probably won't, and check it weekly. For example, you might want to keep tracking slips from packages you mail by Federal Express, Express Mail, or UPS. (Hint: It's usually a good idea to call the recipient on the designated day of arrival just to make sure the package arrived on time and in one piece.) If all's well, you can toss the tracking slips when you check the drawer. One client called this her "Friday drawer" because she found

when she checked it every Friday that most papers she had saved could be thrown away.

REFER: Keeping the Paper Moving

- Create individual "referral folders" for the handful of people you talk to most regularly—your boss, staff, "team" colleagues, etc.—into which you drop things to discuss with that person. Then, at a convenient time, say, "Jim, there are a few things I'd like to go over with you." After you've asked a coworker to get back to you on something, drop a reminder note into his/her folder.

  Your referral folders should be especially accessible; either stand them up in a vertical file holder on your desk or put them at the front of your desk file drawer. You can use colored folders to distinguish your referral folders from other files.
- Or head notebook pages with the names of those same key people and jot down ideas to discuss as they occur to you. Then catch each person at a convenient moment and go over your list.
- Using the referral folder principle, create automatic agendas for your regular meetings. For example, drop materials to be discussed at Monday's staff meeting into a folder headed "Monday Staff Meeting," and add to it as things come up. By Monday you've collected an instant agenda!
- At home, create a "spouse basket": Put all papers to discuss with your spouse—an invitation, your child's report card, a message from your insurance agent—into a single basket. Talk things over daily and clean the basket out. Try discussion baskets with your kids too.

ACT: Getting Things Done

A key obstacle to action is getting caught in the "low-priority trap"—you push aside a piece of paper such as an alumni bulletin, thinking, "This isn't pressing, I'll just look at it tomorrow . . ." Before you know it, "tomorrow" is three weeks later, and those seemingly unimportant pieces of paper have accumulated into a dark, dense thicket of daunting decisions. What to do? Deal with it! If a piece of paper is worth saving, it's worth acting on—and soon.

The five keys to getting through your action stack

1. Set a regular half hour every day for TRAFing and working through your action stack. Stick to the time limit. Some people prefer to hold paperwork (except for urgent matters) until late in the day or early the next morning so they can deal with it while the phones are quiet.
2. Thumb through the stack quickly and take note of those tasks that require a substantial time commitment. Then pick a realistic time to work on them and enter it into your calendar. For example, you know it will take an hour or two to go over the new newsletter layout, so pencil in an hour at 3:00 this afternoon, and an hour tomorrow at 11:00.
3. Riffle quickly through your action stack a second time and pull out two or three top priorities. Act on those tasks first, then work through the rest of the stack in the order that it falls. And if *everything* seems like a priority? Then work through the stack in order. *Don't shuffle pieces of paper around.*
4. You are about halfway through your action stack and already you are in a paper panic. Perhaps there's one item that's really bugging you—you know you need to make a decision, but you just can't think about it now. *Decide* to think about it later—don't just push it aside. Mark it with a red dot and move on. If any document gathers three red dots, that means you've passed it by for three days and it automatically gets pushed into red alert. It should be dealt with at once.
5. When your TRAFing time runs out, stop, even if you haven't gotten through your action stack. Start tomorrow's session at the bottom of the stack and work up, so old business gets cleared up first.

Two-Step TRAFing

Perhaps you've received a letter which would be better handled by another party—someone in a different department, for example. In a situation like this, you need to take two-step TRAFing action. First, act on it—call the sender to confirm receipt or send a note of acknowledgment. Then refer the letter to the other, more appropriate party.

Three variations on working through your action stack

The "right" way to work through your action stack depends largely on your individual style. While it's usually best to tackle priority tasks first, the feeling of accomplishment you get from plowing through busywork may motivate you to confront your priorities with energy and confidence. Here are the alternatives— just be sure to keep deadlines top-of-mind and plan your time accordingly.

1. Do priorities first. This is the best bet for anybody with a consistently heavy paper load. Save busywork till last.
2. Do busywork first. Says one magazine executive, "It clears the decks and the brain." *Caution:* Don't get so involved in the side issues that you never get to the main event.
3. Work from the top down. Begin at the top of your action stack, and work straight down.

Tips for moving paper in and out fast

- Handwrite your reply at the bottom of a letter or memo and pop it back in the mail to the sender that very day! Handwriting is not only fast, it frees you to handle your paperwork outside the office—for example, on the commuter train.

- You can't get any faster than this: Sort and process all mail *with your secretary* daily at an appointed time. (Most people like to consolidate a full day's mail, unless there is a crisis situation.) Working together forces you to make decisions, take action, and delegate as you go.

  Here's how it works: Say a supplier writes you requesting an appointment to discuss a new product. On the spot you decide, first, if you're interested. If so, ask your secretary to call and set up the appointment and enter it into your calendar. If not, dictate a "thanks but no thanks" note to be ready for your signature by day's end.

  Using this strategy, one manager and her secretary were able to process an average day's paperwork in about fifteen minutes. Not only is this method fast, it also forces you to make decisions about things which might otherwise end up in a never-to-be-touched-again pile on your desk.
- Be sure to keep an ongoing follow-up file where you stash things to be dealt with at a later date. Try to come up with a realistic date by which you *must* make a decision. (This concept will be further developed in Chapter 2.)
- At home, keep a basket or file of "quickie" paper tasks, such as recipes for filing, school notes to review, etc., to handle while you're on the phone or while microwaving your frozen waffles. Flip through a catalog while waiting for the water to boil or during the evening news.

Making paperwork easier

- While working on a project, don't stop until you reach a specific goal—for example, finish the opening remarks of that speech you are writing, or finish the budget section of that report before you leave for lunch. Studies show that if you stop working on a project at an arbitrary point, you probably won't get back to it. A big paper project becomes more manageable if you take at least one step (however small) toward completing it each time you come across that piece of paper on your desk.

Personal Correspondence

Letter writing is increasingly becoming a lost art, replaced by the ease and immediacy of telecommunications, but there is nothing more precious than letters from friends and loved ones.

- To ensure timely thank-you notes, save a couple of samples that you especially like. It'll save you time (and dread) in having to start from scratch.
- For people you keep in touch with regularly—a child at camp, your sister in Portland—keep an open envelope addressed to that person in your desk drawer. Drop in notes, clippings of interest, etc., as you come across them. When the envelope is full, seal it, stamp it, and drop it in the mail.
- Keep a "running" letter, adding a thought or paragraph as it comes to you. *USA Today* reader Bill Grode says, "I usually have two or three letters going at a time," using this method. After six or seven days, throw the letter in an envelope and mail it and keep an ongoing "conversation" going with your friends.

Once you've worked through your action pile and have determined what to toss, what to refer, and what to act on, you will have a pile of papers you'll need to file—and find again. Filing—the final step of TRAF—is one of the most important steps in conquering paperwork gridlock and warrants a chapter all its own. In Chapter 3, we'll get into filing—and how to *find* what you file.

Meantime, here's a Quick Desk Check to do at the end of the day to forestall any new accumulations and ready your desk for tomorrow:

☐   Are all "action" papers in the action box? Put any home-less papers in this box for decision making tomorrow.

☐   Are all papers to be filed in the file box?

☐   Are all papers destined for your assistant or colleagues in the out box or their referral folders?

☐   Are all follow-ups in the holding file (see page 44)?

Four Steps to Unjamming Your Desk and Getting Rid of Backlog

One consoling thought when approaching a jammed-up desk is that by now, you can bet a lot of these papers are obsolete and can be thrown away. (But make sure you answer any memo directly addressed to you, unless it's just too old.)

Here's how to clear things up:

1. Before tackling a backlog, get in a good solid two weeks of TRAFing practice on your current papers to increase your paper proficiency and relieve the terror of tackling paperwork.
2. Ink into your calendar specific times for back-TRAFing: fifteen minutes a day, an hour twice a week, three Saturday afternoons—whatever works for you.
3. Break the burdensome backlog down into smaller, more manageable segments. Pick a small section of your desk—preferably the most critical stack—and dive in. Or start at the lower left corner of your desk and work clockwise around until you've finished.
4. TRAF the first stack you have chosen until you hit desk bottom. Then leave the original area open—you want to create a widening pool of clean, bare desk. Now move to an adjoining stack. Before you know it—and more quickly than you expect—you'll have TRAFed your entire desk.

Setting Up an Efficient Desk and Working Area

A workable physical environment has a great impact on your ability to perform effectively and comfortably. The secret lies in the art of placement: Put the things you use most often where you can lay hands on them most easily.

- If you're right-handed, place your phone on your left, and a pad and pen next to it so you can easily take notes. If you're left-handed, do the reverse.
- Set the three, four, or five files you review most often at the front of your desk file drawer, or keep them in a vertical file atop your desk or credenza. (File away any desktop folders that you consult less than three or four times a week.) Keep reference books within swiveling distance—perhaps on a credenza in back of your desk.
- Make sure your working space has a "clear" look to it. A manager who needed to learn Lotus 1-2-3 was intimidated by the cable jungle around his computer. After removing the cables from sight, he was raring to go.
- Have you ever considered a stand-up desk? Some executives at Prudential Insurance, Kellogg, IBM, Xerox, G. D. Searle, and other corporations swear it reduces fatigue and helps them work more efficiently.

Streamlining and Simplification Tips and Tricks

Standardize basic correspondence

- Standardize answers to routine letters. A dozen form letters will be sufficient to cover a variety of situations. Keep copies of your best letters and paragraphs, and use them as needed.
- Need a quick response to your memo? Add a response line at the bottom. For example: "Do you think we should set up a department-wide scheduling calendar?
  ☐ Yes
  ☐ No
  ☐ Let's discuss further"

Make communications short and tight

Winston Churchill said, "Pray let me have by this evening, on one page [italics added], the status of our tank deployment. . . ." If one page was good enough for Churchill, it's good enough for us. Here are some ideas on making written communications short and tight.

- Procter & Gamble and United Technologies require one-page memoranda. The founder of Hallmark Cards required that memos be written on index cards. He believed, "Any idea which can't be typed on a small card hasn't been sufficiently thought out."
- Keep short memos to the point. Bullet your major points to stay succinct.
- For longer memos and reports:
  —Open with a top sheet that summarizes the issue and your recommendations.
  —Follow with a detailed discussion of the issues.
  —Back up with raw data as necessary: statistics, charts, research, bibliography, etc.

By following this form, you can easily accommodate two distribution lists if necessary: those who will receive the full report, and those who will receive the top sheet only.

Cut down on incoming papers

- Do you need to be on every distribution list you're on? Check through the reports you receive monthly, and request that your name be taken off the list for reports you don't need. (However, if your boss feels strongly about sending you summaries of every departmental meeting, it might be wiser to just toss them.)
- Are you on every junk mail list? Send a stamped, self-addressed envelope to Mail Preference Service, c/o Direct Marketing Association, P.O. Box 9008, Farmingdale, New York 11735, together with a note requesting a free "mail preference" form. This form enables you to remove your name from any or all lists. You can also use it to get *on* selected lists of interest to you.

Make forms more effective

Marks & Spencer, a major London department store, battled excessive paper by scrutinizing every form and file and asking, "What would happen if we threw this away?" Here's what Marks & Spencer looked for:

- Duplicate information
- Extraneous information
- Excessively long distribution lists

In your effort to make forms more effective, be sure to redesign forms so that priority information is prominent. Downplay or remove less important information.

Do's and don'ts of bulletin boards

Papers pinned to the bulletin board can either be very useful or wind up as part of the decor. The basic rule is that bulletin boards are fine for reference papers, but not for action papers.

Do place permanent references on the bulletin board, such as:

- Calendar
- Deadline charts
- Production schedules or workflow charts
- Train schedules
- Inspirational sayings
- Takeout menus

Don't tack up action items or you'll probably never notice them again. Action items are things like:

- Business cards. Staple them to Rolodex cards for easy reference and file them in your Rolodex.
- Tasks and lists of things to do. Transfer them to your action stack.
- Immediate reminders, such as "Call Joe on Thursday." Enter these into your calendar.
- Bills to pay. Keep them in a special folder or basket.
- Special-event schedules, such as football or the symphony. Enter the dates that interest you into your calendar. Use pencil for tentative dates.

Three neat ways to use Post-it notes

- Reminders, reminders everywhere. A Post-it on the front door with the words "theater tickets" written on it will remind you to grab them before you leave the house.
- Posting "Went to the store, be back in 5," on the fridge is a great way to communicate with family members. Keep a filled Post-its holder on the wall with a pen or marker to save you from scrambling through drawers in search of scrap paper.

- Order Post-its with your name on them for short personal notes. (The Horchow catalog, 800/456–7000, is one source.)

Make complex documents simple

- On a separate piece of paper, summarize the key points of a complex document or contract so you won't have to wade through the whole document again. List financial terms, important dates (for example, interim dates and deadlines), and any other items of significance. Don't forget to enter these dates in your calendar.
- Organizer Lucy Hedrick suggests listing contract provisions in two columns—"we" and "they"—for quick access and easy referral. Under "we," list your own obligations and responsibilities, and under "they," the obligations and responsibilities of the other party.

The Paper Test—
How'm I Doing?

How do you know when you're *really* organized? When the papers that cross your desk leave your desk within forty-eight hours.

Here's a simple way to check your skill and invigorate your paper-handling prowess:

- Start noting the date on each piece of paper as it comes in.
- After a week, check every paper on your desk. Give yourself two points for each paper that has been there two days or less, *subtract* one point for every paper that has been there between three and seven days, and subtract two points for anything on your desk that is older than a week.
- Add up your pluses and minuses. Your first goal is to wind up in the black.
- Keep checking each week. Your final goal? All pluses, no minuses. When you attain this level of proficiency, give yourself a reward. Not only have you mastered paperwork, but you will find that your decision-making capacity is strengthened in every aspect of your work.

Do this exercise several times a year to prevent bad habits from creeping up on you.

2

Following Up
and Following Through

Forget about remembering. The cost of forgetting is too high—write it down. And keep track of everything.

Two Easy Follow-Up Methods: The Calendar/ Holding File and the Tickler File

There are two easy ways to help you keep track of what you have to remember:

—the *calendar/holding file* (if you generally have no more than five or six items to follow up on daily)

—the *tickler file* (to be used if you have lots to follow up on every day)

These techniques guarantee that you will never again lose a piece of paper you need, and that you will always be on top of what you have to do and when you need to do it. Here's how each works:

The calendar/holding file method: six simple steps to infallible follow-up

1. Create a holding file—simply write the word "Holding" on a manila folder. That's it. Perhaps you'll want to use a colored folder to differentiate your holding file from other files. Keep it within reach—at the front of your desk file drawer or standing upright on your desk in a vertical file.
2. Estimate a response date for every piece of paper to which you expect a reply. For example, on the 5th you wrote Henry Jones requesting updated sales figures. You think it's reasonable to expect a reply within two weeks, so enter the due date on your calendar. On the 19th jot "Heard from Jones?"
3. Pencil the 19th on your copy of the memo and place it in the holding file for future follow-up.
4. Put the initials "HF," for "holding file," on your calendar next to the reminder, so you'll know at a glance where the material is. *Now you can forget about it* until the 19th.
5. If by the 19th you haven't heard from Jones, pull your copy of the memo from your holding file and follow up. If at first you don't succeed, keep following up periodically until the matter has reached resolution.
6. How about following up on yourself? If you've told someone *you'll* call *them* next week, mark that call date on your calendar and put your copy of any correspondence in the holding file.

The five-step tickler file alternative

If your job requires keeping track of so many follow-ups that the holding file becomes unwieldy, use the tickler file method, as follows:

1. Number thirty-one manila folders 1 through 31, for each day of the month. (Or buy an expanding file folder with pockets numbered 1 through 31 in an office supply store.) Label twelve additional folders January through December.

2. Estimate a response date for every piece of paper you need to follow up on. With this method, you don't need to mark the date in your calendar.

3. Drop the document in the folder labeled with the date you've assigned. If you expect to hear from Jones by the 19th, drop the memo into the folder labeled "19."

4. Each morning, pull that day's folder and handle the day's follow-ups. Remember—if Jones asks you for a few more days, move the letter to the *new* tickler date.

5. If you need to follow up on something next month (or in six months), drop the document into the appropriate month's folder. At the beginning of each month, distribute that month's follow-ups into specific-day folders.

Additional tickler tips

- Here's an idea from H. L. Taylor, author of the book *Delegation:* At the beginning of each month, turn the tickler folders that fall on weekends and holidays backward to avoid scheduling tasks and follow-ups on those dates.

- If your secretary handles your tickler file, here's a tip from Alec Mackenzie, author of *The Time Trap:* In the upper right-hand corner of the document, write and circle the number of days—for example, seven—you are allowing for follow-up. Ask your secretary to file the material under the appropriate date and pull it out for your attention on that day.

Ten additional ways to take advantage of your follow-up systems

1. *Phone calls.* Did Marcia promise to call you next Thursday to confirm your lunch date? Jot it down in your calendar or drop a note in your tickler.* Did *you* promise to call Marcia? Same thing. (Be sure to note Marcia's phone num-

---

* From here on I'll refer only to calendar notations—a note in your tickler will serve the same purpose.

ber in your calendar right next to the reminder so you don't have to look it up again.)

2. *Errands.* The store promised that your suit would be ready in a week. Write a note in your calendar reminding yourself to pick it up.

3. *Requests.* Your vacationing neighbors asked you to pick up the Sunday papers for them. Note it in your calendar.

4. *Assignments.* Your boss asked you to prepare a review of the Maxwell project for a meeting in two weeks. Note the due date, and also the date you should *start* the project to make sure you complete it on time.

5. *Making sure information makes the rounds.* When you send out information with a routing slip, put your own initials last on the list, and note on your calendar the date you expect it back. You can also use this technique with a diskette. Recipients can print or save whatever they need before passing the disk along.

6. *Delegation.* Note benchmark dates and deadlines for assignments given to subordinates.

7. *Tickets and invitations.* Ever get to the ballet or the baseball game, only to remember that the tickets are at home? Place your tickets in your tickler file for call-up on the appropriate date, or write a reminder in your calendar.

8. *Guaranteeing that a project gets done on time.* If you must stop working on a project before it's completed, mark a specific time and date you'll get back to it.

9. *Prescription medicines.* Estimate how long your current supplies will last. Enter a note to reorder about a week before they run out.

10. *Maybes.* Maybe you'll go to the conference in May. Maybe you'll go to your high school reunion. Mark a "decision date" in your calendar. Save any related literature in your holding file.

Sample Routing Slip

TO:

☐ Ellie Michaels   ☐ Lucille Taylor
☐ Chris Muscat   ☐ Henry Wagner
☐ Jim Petrie   ☐ George Welsh
☐ Renee Roberts   ☐ Jack Wilson
☐ Steve Ryder   ☐ Carol Wood
☐ Gary Savarin   ☐ _____

FROM: N. L. Street   Date: _____

☐ For your information/interest
☐ Let's discuss
☐ Please handle
☐ Note and return by _____
☐ Please call me

Using your calendar or tickler to keep track of recurring events

Each year, enter the following reminders:

(*Note:* Since these are recurring tasks, if you use a tickler you can simply list each due date on an index card and as you reach one due date, move the card up to the next.)

Taxes. Enter the following dates: taxes due, estimated payments due, W-2's/1099's expected. Also enter a get-to-work date and a date when materials should be sent to your accountant.

Keogh/IRA. Note date by when contributions must be made.

Birthdays and anniversaries. Impress your friends and family by always remembering special days—and on time. Note birthdays and anniversaries in your calendar. Also enter reminders to send a card or gift a few days early.

- Don't underestimate the small gestures of life. Sending your thoughts via gift or card—and on time—cements good feelings among family members and friends. Make up a master list of important birthdays and anniversaries. When you get your new calendar at the beginning of the year, enter these important dates. Staple the list itself to the last page of your calendar for easy transfer to the following year.
- Mark card and gift purchase dates in your calendar about a week before the actual date and avoid sending belated wishes or doing what I once did—which was to spend major bucks to Express-Mail a birthday card to a favorite aunt. *Or . . .*
- Make a calendar note to card-shop three or four times a year for all upcoming birthdays and anniversaries. Pick up cards at the end of December for January-through-March occasions, and so on. It's great having a card on hand when you need one! (Mark the recipient's name lightly in pencil on the outside of the envelope so you don't forget who it's for—and make sure to erase it before you send it off.)
- Stock up on thank-you and congratulations cards so they're always on hand.

Car maintenance. Enter dates to check your mileage and to have your car serviced.

Insurance. To avoid last-minute panic, jot down renewal dates. Any special questions or changes? Note a date to call your agent a couple of weeks ahead.

Holidays.
- To take the stress out of holiday planning, organize preparations around a time frame, and mark them in your calendar, using the "countdown method": things to do four weeks before Christmas, three weeks . . . , etc. Cross off tasks as you go. Your "Christmas countdown" will save you time and give you peace of mind.

- Create a Christmas-card list the easy way. Tear off the return address from each card you receive and tape to a sheet of paper—you should be able to fit about twenty to twenty-five addresses per page. Photocopy the page for neatness, and make a note on your calendar on November 30 to retrieve your list and start working on your cards.

Other Ways to Follow Up

Meetings: a three-step follow-up plan

1. Prepare a minutes summary of a meeting, listing decisions that were made, who is responsible for carrying them out, and due dates.
2. As each action is completed, mark off on the meeting summary.
3. Put unresolved items first on the next meeting's agenda. As Alec Mackenzie points out, tackling unfinished business first will induce your staff to accomplish their tasks in a timely way.

Complex projects: a four-step follow-up plan

1. On a wide accounting-style ledger sheet, draw thirteen columns—an entry column on the left, and twelve additional columns for twelve weeks of follow-up.
2. In the entry column, name the project, the person you have delegated it to, and the final due date.
3. In the appropriate column, list the tasks that are to be completed within that week and confirm with those responsible.
4. Expect a terse progress report each week. If everything is on schedule, instruct your staff to simply report "on target," and you can check off in your ledger the tasks which have been accomplished. Any glitches or changes require further explanation and recommendations for getting back on track.

3

How to File It— and Find It Again

Some people are phobic about filing, fearful that if it's out of sight it's lost forever—and very often, this feeling is born from fact. Perhaps in the past papers they had put away *were* never seen again. So they keep important papers handy on their desk—until the pile grows to the point where nothing is "lost" but nothing can be found, either.

A good filing system allows you to find whatever you need when you need it and within a few moments. Developing a good filing system is easy, as long as you take it one step at a time.

How to Figure Out What to Name a File

Basic filing fact: It's a lot easier to work with relatively few fairly fat files than with lots of skinny folders with a few sheets of paper in each. The more files you have, the more apt you are to misfile or forget. The most common error is making files too specific! Here are three basic principles for naming files:

The umbrella principle. Use broad, "umbrella" headings that will be easy to remember and that cover a pretty broad chunk of material. For example, combine "Exercise equipment," "Vitamins," and "Arthritis treatments" into a single "Health & fitness" folder.

The sponge principle. Absorb isolated pieces of paper under broad headings. One or two brochures about camera information don't warrant their own "Photography" file. Instead, drop them into a more general file labeled, perhaps, "Hobbies" or "Interests"—whatever works for you.

The personal association principle. Wherever possible, choose the heading that evokes a personal association for *you*. Do your children's booster notices go under "Medical," or in

---

Some Typical Headings for a Home Filing System

Beauty	Schools
Church	Services (plumbers,
Civic activities	electricians, etc.)
Decoration	Shopping (or Stores)
Entertainment	Taxes
Fashion	Travel
Financial*	Valuables
Health & fitness	Warranties & guarantees (for
Insurance	appliances, stereos, VCRs,
Letters *or*	etc. This file includes both
Correspondence	the warranties themselves
Medical	and the instructions)
Memorabilia	
Property	
Restaurants	

Note: You might want to set up individual folders for your spouse and children.

---

* Financial records are discussed in Chapter 6, "The Paperwork of Money," page 74.

files with their names on them? Pick the heading you're most likely to remember, and then be consistent. Just make sure any quirky headings are understood by all who need to use the files.

Three more tips on how to name files

1. Always start a file name with a noun. "New prospects" is apt to get lost. "Prospects—new" can be retrieved easily.
2. File newspaper and magazine clippings by subject. An article about new vitamin therapies goes under "Health & fitness." A file called "Clippings" quickly becomes clutter.
3. "Miscellaneous" is another word for "meaningless." Even those pesky papers you can't quite get a handle on need a permanent home. It's just a matter of coming up with the right association. One client did a masterful job of organizing her filing system, except for three pieces of paper left over: info on a crafts course she wanted to take, a list of novels she wanted to read, and a schedule for aerobics. She realized they all had to do with future goals, so she labeled the folder "Aspirations." Nice.

Special filing categories

- *Directions and maps.* Tired of hearing your friends say, "You need directions *again?* You've been here a million times!" Keep a file of directions to places you expect to return to—you'll save time and effort when you don't have to call and take down the same directions again and again.
- *Photographic negatives.* Place negatives in envelopes and label by date and subject. A shoe box is about the right size for filing negatives.
- *Vacation information.* What was the name of that terrific dude ranch you took the kids to five years ago? And where was that place on the highway that sold great pretzels? Get a loose-leaf notebook and jot down the names of hotels, restaurants, and must-see's. If you like, paste or staple in

one or two brochures from favorite places, then throw the rest of the papers away.

Warranties/guarantees and instructions

Camera conk out? Refrigerator on the fritz? If only you could find the warranties! And what about the instructions for your four-year-old's injured "action" gizmo? Here are some ways to keep these important materials easy to find when you need them.

- Set up a single "Warranties and guarantees" file, and be sure to include product instructions. Use a folder with *closed sides* to keep all those odd-sized pieces of paper from falling out. Attach your sales receipt to the warranty, and if the item was a gift, note when it was received, and if possible, where it was purchased. *Or...*
- Use envelope-style dividers in a loose-leaf notebook. File warranties and instructions alphabetically by the type of appliance (dryer, television, VCR, etc.) This alternative requires a bit more effort to set up, but the reward is quicker, even easier accessibility than the single-file method mentioned above.

Setting up new files

- It's usually not a good idea to start a new file with fewer than four or five items on a topic unless you anticipate it

---

How Long Do I Keep . . . ?

- Phone messages—one year.
- General correspondence—two years.
- Contractual and other legal documents—indefinitely.
- Tax documents—six years.

will grow, i.e., you registered for night school, you're getting married, etc. In these cases, create a file as soon as you start accumulating information. (As always, choose headings according to the umbrella, sponge, and personal association principles.)

Subdividing unwieldy files

When a file folder becomes too unwieldy, you may need to subdivide the information into separate folders. There are three ways to do this:

By bulk. When the material is very general and not time related, simply create an additional file with the same name, and divide the material up evenly. For example, a social worker in criminal justice collected masses of paper on legal resources. When the file became too thick, she broke it up into "Legal resources I" and "Legal resources II."

By topic. You've accumulated several items on fax machines in your "Computers & electronics" file and expect to collect more. Pull out that material and start a new folder called "Faxes" or "Fax information."

Chronologically. An unwieldy file of personal letters, for example, could be divided by date: Letters '97, Letters '98, etc.

Your Vital Documents Checklist

It's a fact of life that the critical events of our lives—birth, marriage, purchase of a home, death—are trailed by reams of paper. These are the documents you would be lost without.

These are your "paper valuables" and should be treated as carefully as you would jewelry or silver. Store these valuable documents in a safe-deposit box or fireproof safe. It's also wise to make copies of the most critical documents and store them in another location—perhaps your lawyer's office. List the names of the documents and their whereabouts, and give one copy of the list to a family member or trusted friend, and send one to your lawyer. This list should include:

Auto titles, receipts of purchase, and car-servicing records. Keep a file of receipts for your car, including the original sales receipts and receipts for service. If you've been servicing your car faithfully, you might get a higher price when it comes time to sell it or trade it in.

Bank account information. Record account names, numbers, signers, and banks.

Consulting professionals. List names and addresses of attorneys, accountants, brokers, insurance agents, bankers, etc.

Credit card information. Keep a list of all your credit card numbers at home and in a safe place at the office. As a backup, photocopy the faces of all your credit cards. You might also consider registering your cards with a consumer-protection service. If your cards are lost or stolen, the service reports it to your credit card companies and arranges for new cards.

Home improvements. Keep a file of all receipts for repairs and remodeling you have done on your home, including charges for materials and labor. These records can affect your tax situation when you sell your home.

Home inventory. Keep a room-by-room inventory of significant furniture, accessories, antiques, silver, and artwork, listing place of purchase, date, serial number, and purchase price. It's a good idea to have photographs taken of valuable pieces to support insurance claims.

(Continued)

Insurance policies. For each policy, list type (auto, fire, homeowner's, life, liability, etc.), insurer, agent or contact, number and date, key provisions (optional but wise), and expiration or renewal date, if any.

Legal documents. Protect your leases, powers of attorney, incorporation or partnership instruments, contracts, and certifications.

Mortgages and purchase records. All documents related to the purchase of your home and other real property documents should be included.

Personal records. Store birth certificates, marriage license, divorce papers, passport, military papers, naturalization papers, etc.

Safe-deposit box access. List other individuals (such as your spouse or grown children) who have access to the box in case of emergency.

Securities. Include negotiable securities, trust papers, and information on Keogh, IRA, and pension plans.

Tax returns and supporting materials. Keep all supporting materials (canceled checks, receipts, bills, etc.) for six years in case of audit. In complex tax situations, check with your lawyer or accountant.

Warranties and bills of purchase for major items. Make a list of appliances and electronic devices by brand, model, serial number, place of purchase, date of purchase, and warranty information.

Will. Keep the original with your lawyer and at least one copy at home. *Note:* Never keep the original in a safe-deposit box, which may be sealed upon death.

Making Files Easy to Find and Keep under Control

Alphabetize

- It's usually best to file every folder in strict alphabetical order. Once again, remember to start file names with a noun.

When a paper applies to more than one file . . .

You have a choice. You could:

- Duplicate it. An article on restaurants in Chicago could be filed in "Restaurants" and also in "Travel." *Or . . .*
- Cross-reference it. File the article on Chicago restaurants in "Restaurants," and drop a note (i.e., "See article on Chicago in restaurants file") into the Travel file. Consider jotting your cross-reference note on colored notepaper. You may also want to cross-reference via *folder*. For example, if you never remember whether you filed car insurance papers under "Insurance—Car" or "Car Insurance," why not make a folder for both headings, file the papers in one and put a cross reference note in the other.

Use color-coding

- You can quickly lay hands on your most important papers by using different-colored file folders. Choose colors by association: red for medical records (Red Cross), blue for financial matters ("blue chip"), green for bills to pay. Choose your own color associations—it's kind of fun.
- Use different-colored file folders or file labels to distinguish active project files from reference files.

Keep your files visible

- If you're one of those people who need your files in sight to feel secure, keep them visible. Set up long bookshelves and store your files upright in clear plastic file boxes so you can see them all at a glance.

"Fingertip storage" for most-used folders

- Keep most-used folders at the very front of your file drawer, separate from your regular A-B-C files. *Or...*
- Remove most-used or critical files and keep them close at hand in rolling carts or mobile caddies.

File index

- To keep track of files, make an alphabetical list of all your folders and tape it to the side of the file cabinet. Update by hand until it gets messy, and then print out a fresh copy.

Keep files lean

Files have a way of growing like weeds, and like weeds they need to be cut back. Here are some suggestions for file control.

- Each time you open a file folder, flip through it quickly and toss out any deadwood that jumps out at you.
- Set firm limits on space allocations for your files. John Curley, CEO of the Gannett Corporation, comes in on a Saturday afternoon once or twice a year and—with one eye on the ball game—weeds his deskside files back to about half.
- To get rid of a backlog, weed through six files each day. Put the six files on your desk the night before, and spend fifteen minutes on them first thing the next morning.

Messy file buildup?

- Pick a day and time once a week when you (and/or your secretary) plow through the filing.
- To keep a heavy filing load under control: In an expanding alphabetical folder, drop each piece of paper to be filed into the slot for the appropriate letter of the alphabet. Then file two or three letters' worth every day. For example, "Today I'll catch up on the G's and H's."

Seven steps to reorganizing a filing system

You'll know it's time to reorganize when you can't find anything you've filed. Here's how to do it:

1. Set regular reorganizing appointments with yourself. Plan to get in a half hour early twice a week, or instead of going out for lunch, have a sandwich at your desk.
2. Take out one folder at a time and toss out the deadwood. Send folders you feel confident you won't be using to storage without bothering to sort through them.
3. Evaluate each file heading according to the three file-naming principles (umbrella, sponge, and personal association) on pages 50–51. Don't forget to begin names with a noun.
4. Consolidate thin folders, and subdivide excessively thick ones, following the principles on page 54.
5. Place the folders back in the file in alphabetical order according to their new names.
6. As you go along, list each file name alphabetically on a sheet of paper. When the file reorganization is complete, this will form your file index.
7. Tape up your file index or keep it in a binder on top of the file cabinet.

Addresses and Business Cards

Getting extra mileage from your Rolodex

Card address directories—generally known as Rolodexes for the best-known brand—are still among the most versatile and efficient tools around for organizing your contacts and other information. Here are some Rolodex ideas.

- I recommend the flat-tray 3″ x 5″ model to avoid "card fallout," which frequently occurs with the roller type. This larger-size card gives you room to note birthdays and other information. (Be sure to also copy the names and numbers you refer to most often in an address book that you can carry with you.)

- Use your Rolodex as a handy information resource. Note a colleague or client's complete title and assistant's name, and any relevant personal information such as birthday, spouse's name, etc.
- Make a single "airlines" card, listing phone numbers, your frequent flier numbers, and airline clubs you belong to.
- You can also make travel cards for the cities you visit most frequently. If you often fly to San Francisco, make a San Francisco card listing your preferred flights, favorite hotels and restaurants, and clients and contacts in that city.
- Write directions to a contact's home or office on the reverse of his/her Rolodex card.
- Overstuffed Rolodex? Try this: Divide cards into three categories: (1) active contacts, which you keep in the Rolodex; (2) inactive contacts, which you can store in an index-card box for future reference; (3) obsolete contacts—which you can throw away.

Addresses the electronic way

- Keep your address book on your computer. Print it out and keep it in your diary planner or a small loose-leaf notebook. Leave enough space between addresses so you can update by hand. When changes accumulate, enter them into your computer and print out an updated fresh copy.
- A hand-held organizer such as the Sharp Wizard will easily hold hundreds of addresses—and you can carry it with you wherever you go.

Business cards

Business cards are pesky things whose usefulness declines in direct proportion to their volume. You can, however, turn these cards into sources of valuable information.

- When you receive a business card, write a reminder to yourself: Note who the person is, the date and circumstances of your meeting, and any mutual contacts. You might even want to follow up with a "nice to meet you" note.

- If your software has a "contact manager," enter the same information, and also the person's occupation and any other data you like. So if you vaguely remember meeting a graphics designer last year, and now you're in need of one, press the keyword "graphics" and that reference will pop right up.

- Before you hand out your own business card, write a personal note of reminder on the face of the card: "Enjoyed meeting you at the sales conference 11/2," or "Be happy to give you a company tour next time you're in town."

- Sort business cards into two categories: Active contacts are people you want to keep in touch with; "maybe somedays" are exactly that.
   —Alphabetize each card in the active group by name or firm, and staple it onto a card in your Rolodex.
   —File the "maybe someday" group simply under *A, B, C,* etc. Don't bother alphabetizing exactly. Store them in a small business-card box you can purchase at a stationery store. Or, drop business cards into a file folder labeled "Contacts." Just be sure to use a file folder with closed sides so the cards won't fall out.

Keeping stores and services at your fingertips

- Set up your own classified phone directory in your address book or Rolodex as you collect often-used numbers. (Why not use yellow Rolodex cards to signify "yellow pages" for easy identification and retrieval?) Organize services by category. If you collect antiques, keep all dealer cards together under the letter *D* and write the word "Dealer" at the top of each card. "Furniture restorers" and "Appraisers" would also be put together.

- If you tend to think of a firm by its name, list it that way with a cross-reference to its category. You might enter "Acme Cleaners" under *A,* and also under *C:* "Cleaners—see Acme."

4

Organizing a Home Office

Your home office can be that table where you pay bills, or an entire room devoted to running a full-fledged business. No matter how small or large, your home office is an important nerve center and requires careful planning for maximum comfort and efficiency.

Choosing an office location

Most people have limited space, and there are only one or two places where they can locate a home office. But others have lots of options. These questions will help you pinpoint the best location for you to work.

☐ Do you work best with the sun streaming in, or are you a low-light person? Different rooms receive varying amounts of light at different times of day, and it's important to keep that in mind, along with your peak performance hours.

☐ Do you like being near windows, or do they distract you?

☐ Are you better "in solitary," or do you prefer being near other people?

☐ Is there enough space for a desk, computer, and other equipment?

☐   Is the area pleasant? That grungy area near the furnace in the basement may be the obvious choice, but is it the best choice if the time you spend there is going to be a downer?

☐   Is there access to electrical outlets and telephone jacks? If not, can they be readily installed?

☐   Are you a morning, afternoon, or evening person? If, for example, you work best at 11:00 P.M., you'll need to find a spot that won't disturb the household. Conversely, if you shine at your household's busy time—when your kids are doing their homework, your spouse is coming home, the TV is on—the living room may not be the best choice. It's important that the place you choose work for your family's schedule as well as your own.

Creating a desk and office area

• Let your kitchen do double duty. All you need is a kitchen countertop, a drawer, a stand-up file, and a nearby telephone. Keep notepads, stamps, and other supplies in the drawer, and keep bills, warranties, school papers, etc., in your stand-up file. *Or . . .*

• Turn your bedroom into your boardroom. A theatrical agent I know who loves working from bed covered a large lucite board in fabric to create a lap desk—and has done some of her biggest deals there! If you choose this route, you will also need a night table or bedside caddy—a fabric pocket that hangs from the side of your bed—for your supplies. You can attach the caddy to the bed by anchoring a long fabric strip under your mattress. With a phone, address book, and calendar, you're ready for a productive morning. *Or . . .*

• Place a wooden butcher-block slab over two two-drawer filing cabinets to create a full-sized desk, and keep your files at your fingertips. Just be sure you've got enough space for a full-sized desk *before* you purchase the slab.

Office Supplies Checklist

The supplies listed below are the basics you will need to keep your home office humming. Whenever possible, buy items in quantity—you'll not only save money, but you'll also save the aggravation of running out of supplies. A box of 500 sheets of white paper, a couple of boxes of diskettes, and two or three boxes of pens should last awhile.

Keep an eye on your inventory. Note the items you are running low on in your notebook, and purchase new stock when convenient.

Address book and/or Rolodex
Bulletin board, or several squares of stick-on cork
Business cards
Calculator
Calendar/planner
Carbon paper, if you use a typewriter. *Hint:* The most convenient kind is "copyset" carbon paper—the backup paper is attached to the carbon, which is torn off and thrown away.
Clipboard
Computer disks and storage containers
Computer paper and supplies
Copier paper and supplies
Desk clock
Desk lamp
Dictionary, and other references: airline guide, etc.
Erasers
Fax paper and supplies
File folders. Letter-size folders are easier to handle than legal size. In either case I suggest "third cut" folders, in which the stick-up tabs are staggered for easy viewing.
File folder labels
File rack for desktop files

Hanging files (Pendaflex). Many people prefer them, but bear in mind that they are more expensive and take up more space than manila files.

In box and out box

Index cards

Letter opener

Mailing labels

Mailing/package tape

Manila envelopes and Jiffy bags (padded envelopes to protect fragile packages)

Marking pens and highlighters in different colors

Pads: personalized memo pads, plain small pads for odd notes, larger legal- or letter-size pads

Paper clips, regular size and oversized

Pencil sharpener. If you are a serious pencil user, I suggest a battery-operated desk model.

Pencils and pens

Post-it notes (colored stickies) in assorted sizes

Postage scale (small), for oversized mail

Prop, to hold a sheet of paper that you are retyping

Rubber bands, mixed sizes

Ruler

Scissors

Scratch paper: inexpensive pads for drafting letters and writing down thoughts

Scotch tape and dispenser

Stamps. Also keep appropriate postage on hand for international mail and other special mailings if you do them regularly.

Stapler, staples, staple remover

Stationery and envelopes. Full-sized (8½" x 11") letterhead stationery, matching business-size (#10) envelopes, and smaller notepaper for handwritten notes

Telephone. Install an extension at your desk, or consider a cordless phone. If you do extensive work on the phone, consider purchasing a telephone opera-

(Continued)

tor-style headset. It will free your hands and ease neck and back strain.

Typewriter and supplies: ribbons, correction fluid (e.g., Wite-Out). Most computerized offices still keep a typewriter on hand for short notes, addressing envelopes, filling out forms, etc.

Typing paper

Wastebasket

Some neat ideas on where to store things

- Designate a spare shelf for your laptop, files, and supplies.
- Your "Born to Win" mug, or the ceramic vase your son made in school, is handy for holding pencils and pens.
- Inexpensive plastic containers or mesh vegetable baskets can hold paper, supplies, diskettes, and computer gear.
- Wheeled storage bins on runners are particularly handy when a room, like your kitchen, is pulling double duty. When you're through for the day, you can wheel your office out of the kitchen and into a closet.
- Wall organizers are a real space saver. You can purchase these molded plastic units that hang on the wall for pads, pens, your calendar, and other current supplies.

Mail and postage tips

- If you have a heavy volume of mail, buy stamps in several denominations to allow for outsize pieces, and invest in an accurate postage scale. Also be sure to buy stamps in rolls of 100 so you won't constantly be running out.
- While you're watching TV, make up mailing labels with your return address to save you time when you really need it. Use a laser printer, typewriter, or, if you've got pleasant, legible handwriting, print labels carefully. You can also have mailing labels printed by a professional for a nominal charge.

- It's stamped, sealed, and now you decide you don't want to deliver. Or, perhaps you just discovered you've written the address upside down. Believe it or not, you can retrieve the stamp. Simply press the stamp against a damp sponge, carefully lift it off the envelope, and place it at once on a fresh envelope before the glue has a chance to dry.
- Ever have an envelope seal itself without your permission? To unstick it, try putting it in the freezer for half an hour.

Useful Little-Known Facts

- Play-Doh, which is available in most toy stores and in some drugstores, is a neat way to clean computer or typewriter keys: Just work it on top of and around the sides of the keys. Then remove, and your keys are dust-free.
- Need to measure something quickly? A dollar bill is 6 1/4″ long.
- Don't you hate it when you cut your gift wrap an inch short? Here's a quick and simple measuring technique: Wrap a string around the package first, and then use it to measure your paper.

5

Reading Expeditiously— Zipping through Newspapers, Magazines, and Catalogs

Are those piles of newspapers, magazines, and catalogs threatening to dispossess you? You *can* harness the onslaught and regain control of what you read. Three-foot stacks of unread magazines can be reduced to a few manageable inches if you employ three simple principles:

1. *Focus.* Be specific in your choices.
2. *Set a time.* Find it or make it.
3. *Use it well.* Read effectively and efficiently.

Choose which magazines to read, don't let them "choose" you

- When was the last time you actually read *National Geographic?* Which periodicals offer the most information or value per unit of reading time? Check your subscriptions and ask yourself, "Do I really need and read this magazine?" If not, cancel it.
- Another option is to "cycle" magazines. A book editor I know *always* reads *Publishers Weekly* but cycles other publishing journals, subscribing to one or two one year, and a different one or two the next.
- Rather than tossing old magazines, or recycling them, donate them to a local school, hospital, or nursing home. Don't forget catalogs—they can be fun reading too.

Rip and read

- Use the table of contents. Instead of flipping through the magazine, where your attention might be diverted by articles that are less useful, *choose* what has value to you by marking them in the contents. Tear out the articles you choose, and discard the rest of the magazine. If you need to save the whole publication, and/or other people read it, photocopy the articles you're interested in, or mark the pages on the front cover.

Lessen your newspaper load

- Pull out specific pages or sections to read. One executive tears out and reads only the front page and the editorial page of *The Wall Street Journal* every day. She saves the rest of the paper for twenty-four hours in case she wishes to read the rest of an article, and then discards it. *Or . . .*
- Check the newspaper summary of contents and mentally rate each piece. Then read in full only the articles that rank 7 or greater on an interest scale of 10.

The art of clipping

One reason why stacks of newspapers accumulate so quickly is that you're saving them to clip interesting articles—someday. Funny how that day never seems to come. When you can't clip right away, try one of these techniques:

- Tear now and clip later. I'm an inveterate article-clipper. I tear out the pieces I'm interested in as I come across them, and clip the edges later when I have scissors handy.
- When tearing isn't practical—perhaps you're in a public place, or your spouse hasn't read the paper yet—tear off a corner of the page so you can easily find it later. *Or . . .*
- Mark on the front page the page numbers(s) of the article(s) you want to save.

- For clipping ease at home, prepare a clipping kit comprised of scissors, small stapler and staples, pen, and highlighter, and keep it with your "to clip" stack. Clipping is great when watching TV, talking on the phone, or listening to music.

To avoid having to read a piece a second time

- As you read, highlight the sections of the article that you may wish to refer to again.

Four ways to make time for reading

1. Carry articles you've clipped in your briefcase or bag to make good use of time spent waiting at the doctor's office, pharmacy counter, or in line at the supermarket.
2. Read when you travel. Whether it's a long airplane flight or a local commute on the train, bus, or subway, travel time is great reading time.
3. Glance through an article or two during TV commercials, or while waiting for the water for the pasta to boil.
4. Do you and your spouse both like to read the newspaper and some of the same magazines? Use driving time together as a chance for the nondriver to read out loud for the both of you.

File first, read later

- Here's a terrific time-saver: Rather than save countless unscreened articles to read "as soon as you get the chance," often you can preread just enough of the piece to know if it's worth saving. If so, clip and file it to read later when the need to know arises. For example, if you come across a long piece about inns on Chesapeake Bay, file it in "Travel" to read when you're ready to plan a trip.

To find a specific article in a back issue

- You're ashamed to admit it, but you've saved every *National Geographic* for the last seven years—and now you are actually going to Borneo and need to find that article you read a year ago. Here's a way to keep track of exactly what's in your magazine library. When you get your magazines each month, take a few minutes to tear out or photocopy the table of contents and put it in a folder in chronological order. This will serve as a guidebook to your archives, and you will have made quick work of finding an elusive article. To ensure that you will find what you are seeking, index only those magazines that contain subjects of enduring interest to you. Indexing every magazine indiscriminately only defeats your purpose.

Three ideas for getting more out of your reading in less time

1. Invest in a speed-reading course. The payoff will be time saved scanning memos, reports, and books.
2. Skim newspaper headlines and read only the first few paragraphs to get the who, what, when, where, why, and how.
3. For lengthy reports, read the intro, the conclusion, and the first sentence of each paragraph to get the meat of it.

Five techniques for getting the most out of a book

Falling behind on the best-seller list or other books of interest? Try these five useful techniques for summary reading from Alan Lakein's time-management classic How to Get Control of Your Time and Your Life:

1. Read the book jacket carefully to get a good sense of what the book is about. Then examine the table of contents, checking off chapters of particular interest.
2. The first twenty to fifty pages should introduce the author's thesis or school of thought. Read with highlighter in hand to note any key passages.
3. Then read the chapters you checked off in the table of contents.

4. Turn to the index to see if there are topics of interest that weren't included in the chapters you read.
5. Read the final twenty to fifty pages for the author's conclusions.

Not another catalog!!!!

Does it seem like you are on every mailing list in the world, and in some cases, twice? You can *help save a small forest—not to mention some much-needed personal space—and still enjoy your catalogs.*

• At the mailbox toss the tofu catalog and the grass-seeds-of-the-world brochure, and quickly flip through the others, tearing out the pages with items that might interest you. Also pull out the order form. Then and there, throw the rest of the catalog away (or in your recycling bin). When you get inside, staple the pages together and put the packet in your "bills to pay" box or basket.

   If, after paying your bills, you find there's money in the kitty for catalog purchases, go through the pages you pulled out and order your selections. *Or . . .*

• If you're a catalog connoisseur who prefers to pore over pages in search of a special gift or bargain, just be sure to keep your catalogs updated so you don't waste time studying bygones. Stack them in alphabetical order in a stand-up magazine rack by your favorite chair. When the next L. L. Bean or Sharper Image comes in, replace the old with the new and toss the old immediately. Keeping them by the phone and your favorite chair lets you browse through the stack comfortably during long conversations.

• Maximize your time by ordering during off-hours. Most catalog houses maintain twenty-four-hour 800 numbers, and the lines are much less busy at 10:00 P.M. or midnight. Once you've ordered, note the date and put the pages with the items you have ordered circled into a file folder. As the items arrive, check to make sure they're the right size, color, and listed price, then file the pages in a permanent file called "Catalog orders" for future reference. You may not recognize your favorite turtleneck in next fall's Lands' End catalog, but if you keep the catalog pages you can quickly call up its style number and color code. This tip eliminates the possibility and hassle of reordering the wrong thing.

6

The Paperwork of Money: Making Short Work of Bill Paying and Taxes

Four steps to making bill-paying simple

1. Keep unpaid bills, along with stamps, envelopes, and calculator, together in a file or basket. (How about choosing a distinctive color—green?—to distinguish it from other files?)

2. Choose one person in your household to regularly act as banker. The banker will deposit checks in the bill-paying account and pay the bills.

3. Set a regular monthly date to pay bills and balance your checkbook. *Or* ...

   To keep your money working for you as long as possible, write the due date on the envelope of each bill and pay only those near due to save time and money. This works only if you follow the system scrupulously, because if you get careless, you could be face with a run of overdue charges.

4. After you've paid your bills, file the bill stubs and bank statements. The simplest way: Drop them into an expanding folder organized by month, and discard after one year. It's wise, however, after the year is up, to transfer bills and receipts for major items, such as appliances, to a file labeled "Household" in your general system, and keep them for the life of the product. Filing bills is more involved if you itemize income-tax deductions. See pages 75–76.

Those pesky credit card slips

• Put your credit card slips into envelopes labeled with the names of your credit cards—American Express, Visa, etc. When you receive your bill, check your receipts against the items on your bill to make sure it's accurate. Then throw the slips away (unless you are saving them for tax purposes —in that case, see below).

Making tax preparation less painful

When it's that time of year again, you don't have to start popping antacids. The following four-phase system will go a long way toward reducing tax-time anxiety, whether you use a tax preparer or do it yourself. A well-organized tax system can save you time and money, and will relieve unnecessary anxiety in the process.

Phase 1: Setting up your system

• In an expanding accordion file, label slots according to your deductible categories: charity, medical, mortgage, investments, etc. Also label slots for W-2/1099's, and IRA and/or Keogh plans. As you pay deductible bills throughout the year, drop the stubs and canceled checks into the appropriate slots. (The smaller check-size file is easier to handle than a full-size file.)

• Keep track of deductible mileage on your car in a small notebook in your glove compartment. Record the miles you drive for business, charity, and medical purposes. Also record car maintenance expenses, some of which might be deductible.

• Designate one particular credit card for your deductible expenses to simplify record keeping. Some credit cards send you an annual summary of purchases organized by category—e.g., all restaurant charges for the year are totaled in one column.

• Maintain a diary of your investments. Include purchase price and sale price. Place sales slips and account statements in your expanding folder. Your diary makes simple work of calculating your tax situation.

- Have you made capital improvements to your home? Keep all records and receipts in your *regular* filing system in a folder labeled "home improvement." The records might save you taxes when you sell your home. Also keep expenses connected with the closing, such as title insurance and legal services, in the same file.
- Mark due dates for estimated tax payments in your calendar about a week *before* the actual date to give you a few days to prepare and send your estimated tax form and check.

Phase 2: Getting ready

- Though the IRS automatically sends you most of the tax forms you normally use, it's wise to make sure that you have all the forms you need, including those for self-employment income, investment income, etc. There are also forms for noncash charity contributions, an office in the home, and other special situations. Remember to pick up extra copies or photocopy your originals for "working copies."
- Around the end of January, schedule a few working sessions to add up all accumulated bills, receipts, and investment statements. To avoid getting overwhelmed, break the job down: For example, on Monday, add up your pay stubs to make sure they correspond to your W-2; on Tuesday, add up charity donations, etc. If adding 2 + 2 throws you into a tailspin, delegate adding-up chores to the math whiz in the family, or to a trusted friend who owes you a favor. The person you *don't* want doing the adding is your accountant. Let your accountant's meter run for more complicated tax tasks.

Phase 3: Doing them

- Enter a "must start" date in your calendar, and stick to it. Also enter dates for sending materials to your accountant. The earlier the better!
- If you do your own taxes, you'll need these materials: in addition to your clean copy, "working" copies of tax forms;

scratch paper for figuring; calculator; your list of tax deductions and other figures (which you have already prepared, right?); and a tax guide for reference. I find it's easier to bite the bullet and designate an entire day to fill out all the forms, rather than break the task up.

Phase 4: Finishing up and filing away

- Make up a file labeled "Taxes" in your general filing system. Place a duplicate of your completed forms there. Make an additional folder headed "IRA" or "Keogh" for duplicates of those documents.
- Put a copy of your filled-out forms, along with receipts, bills, canceled checks, and other documentation—in a manila envelope marked on the outside with the year. Toss it on the top of your highest closet or in the bottom of your deepest chest. You'll only need it if you are audited.
- I'm often asked, "How long do I need to keep my tax records?" In most cases, the IRS does not audit returns more than three years old, but in some cases, returns are audited up to six years later or longer. So just to be safe, it's wise to hold on to these manila envelopes for six years. Confirm with your lawyer or accountant, who is familiar with your individual situation, before you throw this kind of information away.
- If you're due a refund, mark your calendar, generally a couple of months after your filing date, so you can follow up if there are any delays. The earlier you file your tax return, the earlier you'll receive your refund.

Part Two

GET TIME
ON
YOUR SIDE!

7

How to Set Priorities and Get Things Done

There are just too many things to do, places to go, and people to see—and never enough time for everything. Your proposal is now three days late. You didn't have time to make a crown for your princess's Halloween costume. Your best silk blouse is still at the cleaners, and you are due at the restaurant for dinner in half an hour.

How often do you say to yourself, "Where did the time go?" "If only there were twenty-seven hours in a day," "If I could just get started!" I hear pleas like these from countless clients who are convinced that their lives are too busy and too full for them to take the time to get organized. What they usually fail to realize is that their lack of organization leaves them even less time for their busy lives, and that a small investment now could free up hours of precious personal time for years to come.

Sometimes the culprit is other people: the telephone rings, your mother-in-law drops in, your friend wants to discuss details of her divorce settlement—again. The guy in the office next to yours has a habit of running his ideas by you before presenting them to the boss—which is usually fine, except when you are trying to finish your budget report. Learning to set limits, to say "Not now, later," is key.

And sometimes the culprit is you. If only you hadn't procrastinated on preparing that presentation to the sales staff, you could have really wowed them. You put off sending your aunt a thank-you note for so long that she finally called you in "that" voice to make sure you actually received the candlesticks she sent you for Christmas. And because you haven't cleaned your gutters for the fifth year in a row, you are now presented with a major bill for gutter replacement.

But these situations are not inevitable. I have found that the busiest people often get the most done when they follow two simple rules:

1. *Figure out what is most important.* I have a relative, who is very dear, whose only major flaw is that she assigns the same importance to setting a proper table for tea as she does to solving the problem of world peace. While most of us have a more accurate fix on things, setting priorities is key to protecting and mastering the use of time.
2. *Create your own time plan.*
   • Determine what you have to do and in what order.
   • Figure out when you need to do it by.
   • Schedule the time you need and protect yourself from time wasters (see Chapter 9, "Coping with Interruption Overload," to learn how).

With these rules in mind and the many practical tips that follow, I guarantee that you will have more time to do things, go places, see people—and still have time for a long soak in the tub.

When Two Lists Are Enough: The Master List and Daily List

Lists, lists, everywhere lists. Many people make so many lists that they need a list to keep track of their lists. This approach is more apt to overwhelm than organize you.

It's hard to believe, but you can get it all under control with only two lists—the Master List and the Daily List.

The Master List. This is one of the most powerful organizational tools that exists. It's a comprehensive list of *everything* you have to do. Keep it in one single convenient location, either in a notebook or in a hand-held organizer, and carry it with you at all times.

Simply enter a "to do" in your Master List *as soon as it comes up,* whether it's a report for your boss (and date due), a reminder to buy a new lamp, or a note to get those flyers out for the PTA.

The Master List is a compendium of *all* your tasks, whether you have 10 or 110—a kind of warehouse out of which you move a certain manageable number of tasks each day onto your Daily List.

The Daily List. This is your daily guide to action. It's a separate list, culled from your Master List and other sources, which guides your actions for the day. The Daily List should consist of no more than ten tasks.

Working with Your Master List

How to "operate" your Master List

- Record things that need to be done as they come up. Don't try to "organize" them or set priorities.
- Break big tasks down into manageable "parcels" to avoid feeling overwhelmed. If, for example, you have to write a major proposal, break the work down into several phases, such as (1) write and edit the outline; (2) get input from Jim, Sue, Helen; (3) revise the outline; (4) produce the first draft . . . and so on.
- Each day, check your Master List for tasks you want to schedule at a later time. Enter those tasks onto your calendar on the appropriate day—next week, or three weeks from now —and cross them off your Master List.
- Guess what! Some things on your list just might not be your job. Look through the items and see which tasks can be

delegated. Send notes to your staffers, and cross the tasks off your Master List. You may, however, want to keep track of who's doing what and when it's done, so enter the person's initials and the date assigned onto the Master List.

- Each night, transfer a few items onto tomorrow's Daily List, and cross them off your Master List. A few of these items should be time-pegged—particularly those things you need to get to ASAP. Others should not be.

- Reserve a page of your Master List for major ongoing projects. If you are redecorating, you might have seven to ten things you are working on at one time: looking for a new sofa, redesigning your closets, etc. Try to knock off a few tasks each day. When a task connected with your project first pops up, enter it in the general Master List first so as not to waste time thumbing through your notebook for the proper place. Then rewrite it on the project page during the Master List review.

Some practical tips for Master List maintenance

- Some people are comfortable lumping business tasks and personal tasks together. Others find it easier to distinguish between them, either by using two different-colored notebooks or by sticking a divider tab in their notebook to separate them.

- Only one or two outstanding tasks left on a page? Rewrite them on an active page, crossing off the original entries, to avoid Master List clutter.

- As you complete a page, cut the corner so you can turn easily to the most up-to-date entries.

- As you distribute each task onto your Daily List, calendar, or to staffers, mark the date in your notebook so you'll have a record of it. Keep your Master List notebook for reference for six months to a year.

Variations on the Master List notebook

Master List "masters" have used some of these alternatives to the Master List notebook with great success.

- Use index cards for a lightweight alternative to a notebook. Edwin Bliss finds it useful to carry a half-dozen 3″ x 5″ index cards in his breast pocket. Whenever he gets an idea, he notes it on one of the cards.
- A hand-held organizer, such as the Sharp Wizard or Casio B.O.S.S., offers an additional option for Master List wizardry. Simply enter each task as it occurs to you, as you would with a notebook. The great payoff of the electronic organizer, however, is its ability to recall and sort items by category. You can retrieve phone messages, tasks to be handled by a certain date, and tasks to discuss with specific colleagues by touching just a few buttons. If you also use a computer, get a cable that allows you to hook up your PC to your organizer for even greater ease and versatility.
- You can also enter your Master List on your computer. The "note" feature in many programs allows you to briefly note a task on your Master List, and then stroke a key to call up more extensive background info. The only disadvantage to this is that you can't keep your computer in your pocket. You'll still need a notebook or organizer to jot down tasks that come up when you're away from your desk.

The multifaceted Master List

In addition to being a task list, your Master List notebook provides a handy receptacle for all kinds of information.

- Did your neighbor tell you about a new car-repair place? How about the new salon you read about that specializes in smoothing out unsightly cellulite? Enter them onto your Master List. Also jot down other bright ideas, such as interesting vacation spots you'd like to research, restaurants you want to try, videos you've been meaning to rent, etc. If you don't plan to do anything with this information just now, rewrite it on a piece of paper and drop it into an appropriate file folder for future reference, then cross the info off your Master List.

- Organize your errands geographically—it'll save transportation time *and* the time you'd normally take to figure out what to do when. Head a few pages of your notebook with the general areas in town where you need to go. Then, on the appropriate pages, list stores to check out, museums you've been dying to visit, and errands to run.

- You picked up a terrific idea at a conference or seminar. Highlight it in your notes, and jot down any actions you'd like to take, or issues you need to explore with colleagues, onto your Master List.

- Some people get a bit rattled when they visit their doctor, and the questions they intended to ask go clean out of their heads. List all of your aches, pains, questions, and concerns before you go. Afterward, enter any suggestions or instructions your doctor made, such as "pick up a book on vitamins," or "join an exercise program," onto your Master List.

- Keep a daydream list as wishes occur to you. Maybe your colleague has inspired you with tales of white-water rafting. Your cousin tells you that house prices in Oakdale have just fallen and it's a buyer's market. Enter these items in your Master List. And don't forget about the more immediate pleasures—a trip to see the animals run free at the Bronx Zoo, an antiquing excursion to the country. Jotting down ideas for activities as they occur to you will make for welcome rainy-day reminders.

Working with Your Daily List

The Daily List is your active "to-do" guide, and the key to making it work for you is to keep it manageable. While your obvious goal is to complete all your tasks, it may not always be possible to do so. Don't beat yourself up over it if tasks are left undone. You now have a better grasp of how much you can really accomplish. Remember, you can almost always roll a task over till tomorrow without drastic repercussions.

- Your short list of to-do's should be compiled from your Master List and from tasks that arise during the day. If your day is dominated by breaking events, your Daily List might consist of half Master List and half new tasks. The proportion may change from day to day, but the Daily List should never contain more than ten items.

- To avoid getting overwhelmed, break up larger tasks into smaller bits. "Do the Blackwell report" works for your Master List, but may be too involved as a Daily List task, which instead might read "Do introduction and section on transportation." At home, "Organize tool corner in basement" is a more doable Daily List task than "Clean the basement."

Laying Out Your Day: A Workable Way to Think about Time

Step 1. In the morning, or the evening before, make up your Daily List and set priorities.

Step 2. Get started on the top-priority tasks first thing in the morning. If possible, close your door and protect your time.

Step 3. Raise your time consciousness. Ten minutes here, fifteen minutes there during the day are great opportunities for knocking off midlist and routine tasks such as returning phone calls, jotting down agenda ideas, and, at home, copying the punch recipe your neighbor gave you.

Step 4. Toward the end of the day, look at your Daily List to see what you haven't done, and challenge yourself to finish those few remaining tasks.

Goal: A "no miss" day during which every Daily List item is crossed off.

- A new way to set priorities: Instead of trying to line up priorities 1 through 10, which can hang you up, sort tasks into "priority groups": Place a #1 by your urgent or most immediate tasks, a #2 by the mediums, and #3 by your routine tasks. Important: Try to balance all three categories every day—overloading on #1's may be too ambitious, and the gratification you feel in knocking off a few #3's may motivate you to accomplish more.
- Cross each task off your Daily List as you complete it. Simply roll over any unfinished tasks to tomorrow's Daily List.

Three ways to organize your Daily List

The way you organize your Daily List depends on you. Here are three ways to do it.

Free-form. Don't "organize" at all. Just list tasks randomly. *Or . . .*

By content. Group tasks by subject matter (everything about air quality), location (several customers in one area), or person (several items to discuss with the controller). *Or . . .*

Functionally. Group by similarity of task—for example, all telephone calls, letters to be written, and errands to be run.

When there's a Daily List item you never get around to

- Tackle the worst first, and clear the decks of your most disliked or dreaded task. Said one publishing executive, "I always try to confront the demons up front." You'll feel less stress and can look forward to doing the more pleasant tasks.
- Can someone else do it? If so, delegate. See pages 122–124 for innovative ideas on creative delegation.
- Are you procrastinating perhaps? See pages 106–112 for helpful ideas on mastering procrastination.

- Is it really that important? Maybe it is, but maybe it isn't. Evaluate why you're committed to doing this task, and if your reasons aren't good ones, cross it off your list for good.
- And for those dreaded tasks that just won't quit nagging on your conscience: Peg Bracken, in her *I Hate to Housekeep Book,* suggests writing on slips of paper the miserable jobs you've been putting off (like "Wash the windows," "Tackle filing backlog") and then writing down some fun stuff ("Go to the movies," "Read three chapters of that Agatha Christie novel," "Go bike riding"). Use a 3-to-1 ratio (sorry) of pain to pleasure. Put your slips in a bowl, and a couple of times a week draw one. The sporting spirit will keep you going.

Other Useful Lists

The Master List and Daily List are your basic time-management tools, but other lists can also be useful for reference and in standardizing certain kinds of tasks.

Checklists for work projects. Create a checklist for any projects you regularly undertake. For example, if you run a catering business, list all the steps from signing up the client to cleaning up after the party—and you'll never overlook any important details.

Trips and vacations. Keep a checklist of all pre-vacation preparations, from putting lights on timers to making sure all doors and windows are locked.

Keys and combination locks. List all household keys and combination locks and their locations. Keep the list in a safe place.

Personal documents. Keep a list of valuable documents, such as your will, lists of securities, etc., in a safe-deposit box or fireproof file. See pages 54–56 for details.

The countdown technique for entertaining and holidays. Create a "countdown" party task list: two weeks before, invite guests; one week before, order rack of lamb; etc. This technique can also take much of the hassle and stress out of the holiday season by organizing tasks such as gift buying, decorating, and preparing the holiday meal, into a more manageable countdown format.

Setting Priorities

In *The Time Trap,* Alec Mackenzie said, "I practiced the art of getting more things done rather than getting the few really important things done well." Well-intentioned people sometimes get themselves into trouble by assigning equal importance to buying legal pads and preparing a presentation for the sales staff. Try as we might, the reality of our busy lives forces us to set priorities.

Identifying priorities

What are your priorities? And how do you match time and resources to the priorities you have chosen? Sometimes identifying your priorities out of the myriad claims on your time can be a difficult task in itself. Here are some ideas to help you focus more clearly:

- Your Daily List is gold. Follow the procedures suggested for prioritizing items on your Daily List (see page 88), and do them!
- When all tasks seem equal in importance, ask yourself what's at stake: "How disappointed/distressed/in the hole will I be at the end of the day if I don't get this done?" Put a red sticker by the items that will cause you the most stress if left unfinished.
- Limit your choices and avoid priority overload. Seeking the "ideal" can be paralyzing. Choose only three bakeries, three plumbers, three paper suppliers you want to check out— and then select your preference from among them.

Work toward the high payoff

- Block out time each day for the task that will yield the biggest payoff—a task with potential long-term benefits. Say you'd like to submit an article to a professional journal, which will gain you recognition in your field. Each day, assign yourself one task connected with the project: "Make outline," "Review related material at the library," etc.

Avoid the "low-priority trap"

- Even low-priority tasks require action. Don't fail to knock off these tasks, or they can create a paralyzing thicket of loose ends. Allocate a little time each day to polish them off, delegate them, or swap them with someone else in exchange for a task you prefer. Or, if you can, just cross them off your list.
- To keep your priorities in focus, Alan Lakein suggests that you ask yourself periodically throughout the day, "What's my A?" (Lakein's equivalent of a #1). He uses the example of a harried manager who is stuck on giving one more instruction to his secretary instead of leaving for the airport, even though his flight takes off in forty-five minutes. In Lakein's terms, this manager is indulging in "C-manship," which might result in messing up his most important A—namely, catching the flight.

Set your priorities in motion

- Take a few minutes daily to review your top few priorities for the day and plan when you are going to do them.
- If you have an assistant, ask her to give you a list of what she considers to be your joint priorities for the following day. Go over the list together and then ask her to have the top project on your desk when you come in the next day.

Friendships are a priority too

- Too often in the business of daily life, friendships are rele-
gated to the back burner. Homemaker Jeanette G. Smith
advocates pursuing friendships while doing daily tasks. "My
girlfriends . . . visit while I weed the lawn, fold the clothes,
load the dishwasher." Working on joint tasks makes good
practical use of your time and keeps your friendships alive
and well.

8

Organizing the Day: Figuring Out What to Do When

Organizing your day for maximum productivity is an art. It requires weaving together your personal highs and lows, finding the private time you need to accomplish priorities, as well as responding to the claims of your family, colleagues, and community.

In this chapter you will learn how to "design" your time by setting up the structure that works best for you. Once you define your time parameters, you will be free to brainstorm with coworkers, check your child's homework, and catch that TV special without compromising your own productivity.

Finding Your Peak Time— and Taking Advantage of Your Biological Rhythms

Some of us are morning people, while others are naturally night owls. It is an established fact that we all have an energy curve—times during the day when we are in prime form, and then of course the downtimes. These are your biological rhythms, and ideally you organize certain tasks to coincide with your energy bursts and lapses. One business owner, for example, does his toughest work in the morning, when he's fresh, and saves meetings and easy chores for the afternoon.

Six Ways to Take Advantage of Your Biological Rhythms

When you're at the top of your curve

1. Organize top-priority projects, as well as projects requiring intense concentration and original thinking, to fit into your "high hours."
2. Do you have to confront an unpleasant or stressful task? Ask for a raise or arrange to discuss that poor grade with your child's principal during your high time.
3. Assign routine jobs you dislike to the high hours too. If starting dinner at 4:00 o'clock is a burden to you, organize the meal and set the table in the morning when you are up for it.

When you're at the low end of your curve.

4. Generally, it's best to tackle your #3 low-priority or routine tasks during this time: for example, clipping coupons, folding laundry, paying bills.
5. If you *must* tackle a demanding task during your downtime —for example, if you're required to attend a stressful staff meeting at 4:30—fortify yourself with a high-energy snack. A few spoonfuls of cottage cheese or some nuts and a glass of orange juice about fifteen minutes before the meeting will give you a much-needed boost.
6. Take a break—chat with colleagues, call your spouse, take a fifteen-minute catnap. Or do a few stretching and breathing exercises to invigorate fatigued muscles and trigger those endorphins.

Power-Packing Your Days

Getting a jump start on your day— and other time enhancers

• Ever think of getting a jump start on your day by coming into the office a half hour early? Many of my clients find this gives them much-needed private time to tackle those #1 tasks before the phones start ringing.

- Pencil in specific "appointments" *with yourself* in your calendar for demanding tasks . . . and keep them!
- Scrutinize your "must do" obligations to see where you can borrow time. Can you arrive a half hour late at a work-related cocktail party? And can you duck out early without insulting anybody?
- Book back-to-back family appointments. Make those trips to the dentist, the pediatrician, and the eye doctor on the same day and combine them with some shopping and other geographically related errands.
- Take a late lunch hour and avoid the crowds at the bank and the post office.
- Take a few minutes at the end of the day to get a jump on tomorrow. Something as simple as organizing materials for a meeting enables you to gain some free time tomorrow. You'll be amazed at the feeling of accomplishment you get, even from something small.

"Hidden time"

Most of us have been conditioned to think in terms of nine-to-five. But there are twenty-four hours in a day, and some of my clients have found that organizing their time in other ways has opened up whole new realms of useful and productive time. Said one woman, "I have twenty-four hours to work with. I am free to use any of those hours."

Here are some interesting ideas:

- *By moonlight:* An organizer I know has a client with two small children and a full-time job. She's also going to college. She is coping by going to bed when her children do, by 8:00 P.M., awakening at midnight and doing her schoolwork till 3:00 A.M., and then catching the rest of her winks till 6:00 A.M.
- *By dawnlight:* Organizer Lucy Hedrick talks about "dawnlighting"—using the very early morning hours produc-

tively. Jane Brody, health writer for *The New York Times*, wrote her first book working from 5:00 to 6:30 A.M. every morning.

The benefit of both moonlighting and dawnlighting is that you won't be interrupted by phones ringing and people wandering in. Be aware, however, that not everyone's biorhythms can be conditioned to respond to a schedule like this, which can be grueling.

- *Use "found time":* Do you have a baby who naps? Are your kids upstairs doing their homework (you hope) from 6:00 to 8:00 P.M.? Plan to fit tasks into time slots that other people make available to you.

Six ways to make the most of your calendar

Just as seafarers need a compass, the rest of us need a navigational aid to guide us in our daily lives. Despite many newfangled gadgets, the best tool is still the calendar/planner/agenda, which can be used in myriad ways.

1. Some people try to keep two calendars, one at home and one at the office, but it rarely works—you're apt to book two appointments for the same time slot. It's best to keep only one calendar.
2. As I've mentioned before, your calendar is your most important tool for monitoring and following up. If your client promised to call you next Thursday, mark his or her initials in your calendar. Note the day the notices should go out for the town zoning meeting, and the time of your next haircut. Don't try to remember everything—or anything—let your calendar be your guide.
3. Ever look in your calendar and find "3 P.M. meeting at Sky Club with John Brown," only to realize you haven't a clue where the Sky Club is? When you make the entry, note the address and phone number of your destination. That way you don't have to worry about taking the invitation or meeting notice, and if you're going to be late or if you get lost, you'll have the phone number handy.

4. To make the most of bits of time: Select small tasks from your Master List that you estimate can be accomplished in less than fifteen minutes. Then, when you see an opening in your calendar, plug in one "short goal." For example, if you have some time before picking the kids up from school —not much, but a little—use it the time to hang the dry cleaning in the closet.

5. Have you ever missed an appointment because you forgot to *look* at your calendar? Keep it open where you can't miss it—on your night table, by your phone . . . wherever you'll be sure to see it.

6. Photocopy key pages of your calendar to prevent disaster in case you lose it.

Looking Ahead

Chart your year

- Get a jump on next year by buying next year's calendar in the fall and plotting out the bones of the upcoming year. Enter sales conferences, family vacations, budget deadlines, estimated tax payments—and make a note to make an appointment for your annual physical. Don't forget birthdays and anniversaries.

- Anticipate midseason slump by arranging a special treat and entering it into your calendar. Fight the post-holiday blues by planning a cross-country skiing outing; or beat the heat with a visit to the botanical gardens in the doldrums of August. Entries like these balance your calendar and make days marked with "Do taxes" seem a little less foreboding.

Set goals and plan for the future

- Make a New Year's resolution to set aside a day to set goals for the coming year. Designer Diane von Furstenburg goes off by herself for a few hours on New Year's Day (which also happens to be her birthday) and lists the things she hopes to accomplish in the coming year.

- "Number"-base your goals when possible. One magazine determined it wanted to increase circulation, so it number-defined its goal: "get three out of four distributors in the field to subscribe in the coming year." One PR expert I know determined that a restaurant he represents should be mentioned in the local paper three times a month.

- When mapping your goals, don't forget to include your dreams. Freewheel. Ask yourself what you'd love to do if you were not paid to do it. These "someday" wishes and childhood dreams should include anything and everything, from that world cruise to the karate course you've always wanted to take. Once you commit your goals to paper, even the "daydreams" take on a more serious light.

  Try to schedule at least one of the smaller "I've always wanted to . . ." wishes every week or so. And for your big wish list . . .

- Translate those bigger dreams into reality, over time, by adding them to your Master List. As always, break them down into doable tasks. Interested in building a fortune? One task might be "Read a biography of Andrew Carnegie." Feed those tasks into your Daily List at a rate of one or two a week, and you'll be surprised at how quickly you see your goals taking shape.

9

Coping with Interruption Overload

Private Time without Guilt

It is curious but true that many managers who have little difficulty planning out-of-town trips or attending outside meetings find that carving out private time for themselves *in* the office poses almost insurmountable problems. I often point out to people attending my seminars, "You're out of the office *now*—someone's answering the phones and, yes, business is proceeding."

The realization that things are being taken care of on the home front illuminates the fact that capturing private time is practical when you know how.

The key to making your time your own is to *pinpoint* the time you want to protect.

Trying to protect a whole day is like trying to get your arms around an elephant—you just can't get a grip. *Focusing* your private time is well within range. Here's how:

Five ways to deter drop-in visitors

1. Put a sign on your door: "Hard at work 10:00 A.M. to 11:00 A.M. Glad to catch up with you later. Leave a message with Jane if you'd like a callback." If you work in an open area, substitute a sign on your desk.

2. Position your desk at an angle that avoids automatic eye contact with passersby. This will eliminate the temptation to look up from your work and help you avoid engaging in distracting chitchat.

3. Hide out: Take your work to an unused conference room or a vacant office. One editor with a major newspaper who requires private time for scheduling responsibilities sneaks off to a lonelier part of the office to catch an hour or two undisturbed.

4. Leave the premises: Many mornings, Michael Lester, an attorney, comes into his office, greets everyone, then turns right around and heads for the coffee shop on the corner. There he gains some private time for working on briefs. Other places to which you might escape are the public library, or the park on nice days.

5. Only the "head honchos" can get away with this one: William McGowan, the founder of MCI, had two desks in his large office—one was visible from the door, the other was not. When McGowan was at his "visible" desk, all comers were welcome. But when he was working at his hidden desk, it was the red flag equivalent of "do not disturb."

Three more ways to make more time for yourself

1. Observe the time-honored practice of coming in early and/or staying late. An interesting, little-known fact: The majority of corporate CEOs are at their desks by 7:00 A.M. to do undistracted private work.

2. If a significant portion of your work involves a need for private time, reevaluate your usual schedule: Nine-to-five may not be written in stone. Discuss the possibility of flex-time with your boss. You may find that a simple switch to seven-to-three might be more productive for you and your company. *Or . . .*

3. Can you work at home one or two mornings a week? More executives are spending a couple of mornings a week at home, and are astonished by their productivity.

A *cautionary note: Be accessible.* The flip side of scheduling private time is scheduling accessible time. Otherwise you risk losing touch with the pulse of your organization *and* damaging relationships with colleagues. For the balance of your day: Just as you have scheduled private time, don't forget to schedule accessible time in proportion to your needs—and make your availability known to colleagues.

Making Your Contacts Productive . . . and Crisp

Contacts with colleagues, staff, and clients are a necessary and legitimate part of doing business. The trick is not getting bogged down with inopportune, unscheduled chats in the hallway or on the phone. The following suggestions will help you make the most of the time you spend with your contacts—and move on smoothly.

The fine art of handling drop-in visitors and spontaneous meetings

- *Meet in other people's offices.* When a colleague asks to drop in for a few minutes, try saying, "I'll drop by after lunch." It's a lot easier to excuse yourself from someone else's office than to ease someone out of yours.
- *Set a time contract.* When a colleague asks to see you, say, "Sure, I've got ten minutes at four." Or when you find yourself caught in the corridor with Chatty Charlie, try this one: "I'm really up against it today. We'll need to wind this up in five minutes. If you can send me a memo on the rest, that'd be great." (Chances are, you'll never see that memo.)
- *Confer standing up.* When you want to keep meetings brief, stand rather than sit—standing signals "Don't get too comfortable." Then, when you want to close, simply walk your visitor to the door and say goodbye with a cordial "Thanks for dropping in. I really appreciate the info."
- *Keep your briefcase on the visitor's chair.* This will prevent coworkers from sitting down and overstaying.

Telephone Tactics

Three ways to create phone-free time for yourself

Telephone invasion is among the most insidious of interrupters. A ringing phone almost always compels you to answer—or else!!

1. Freelance editor Margaret Stein controlled the impulse to answer her phone by turning off the ringer and letting her answering machine pick up during her most productive work hours. She became "communicado" again at 11:00 A.M., after having accomplished four hours of solid work.

2. Ask colleagues and friends (and your mother-in-law) to call only at certain times. I know it's hard, but at least try.

3. Have a receptionist or secretary screen your calls, and suggest a time to call back. No secretary? Ask a colleague to do phone duty for you for an hour or so, and tell them you will gladly return the favor.

Avoid telephone tag

- Leave a complete message. Include the reason for the call and any specific information you need to cut down on wasteful backing-and-forthing. A writer and his editor kept exchanging "Call me back" messages. When they finally did connect, it turned out the editor just needed the writer's Social Security number, which could have been easily supplied in a message.
- When the message is "FYI" only, don't forget to add that there's no need for a callback. It's a nice courtesy.
- Delegate as many calls as possible to a secretary or assistant.

But do respond

Streamlining does not include ignoring, forgetting, or "being too busy" to return calls. Responsive communication is the lifeblood of business. Bob Crandall, chairman of American Airlines, will stay in his office until 9:00 P.M. returning all his calls. Many CEOs follow suit, either directly or through an assistant.

- Schedule your callback times as you would a meeting or other appointment. This ensures you will do it, and keeps you from fragmenting your day. Robert Townsend, author of *Up the Organization,* developed this foolproof approach: he had receptionists take all his messages till 11:00 A.M. They then fed them to Townsend, who returned all calls one-two-three within a forty-five-minute period. He found it useful to do this again at 4:00 P.M.

- Make sure *your* calls are returned by leaving a message that requires a response: "Can't move on ordering the equipment you wanted till you give me a price range." It's a lot more difficult to ignore a specific request than it is to ignore "It's Simon. Call me."

Seven ways to make calls short and snappy—without losing friends

1. Opening lines: Avoid "How are you?" because they'll probably tell you, and once they begin, it's hard (and seems more rude) to interrupt. After a "hello," get right to the meat of it: "Rosemary, I knew you'd be the only one who could answer these two questions for me." And if you are the one being called, move in quickly with "And what can I do for you today?"
2. Time your calls strategically. Calls made right before lunch or near quitting time are less apt to turn into chitchat.
3. Set a phone "contract" with your caller: "Hi. Look, I've only got ten minutes, but I really wanted to get back to you." Or alternatively: "Gee, I'd love to talk more with you about this, but I've only got five more minutes. Maybe we can connect later." If your caller is persistent, gently remind them with "That was fast, but I've really got to break now."
4. Here's a desperate measure that's bound to work: When tripped up by a chatty caller, a television producer in Cleveland gives the high sign to a clued-in colleague who yells,

"Jane, you've got a call from London on line one!" and she makes her escape.

5. Stop the action: Jump on the first available pause. Try this at a breath point: "This has been great, Sue, thanks. We'll pick this up at the meeting next week. 'Bye."

6. The frontal attack: You've been nice, you've been polite, but some people just won't take a hint. Say firmly, "I wish I could talk to you longer, but I'm really up against it. I hope you don't mind." Make the statement in a matter-of-fact voice, then hang up immediately.

7. To handle the inveterate chatterer, you may have to limit telephone contact or avoid it altogether by substituting memos or E-mail for the telephone.

How about getting yourself off the phone?

• If *you* have a tendency to chatter, you might try this trick: A hotel manager kept three three-minute egg timers on his desk, and turned one over when his conversation started. His goal: as many one-egg-timer conversations as possible. Some calls, of course, legitimately lasted two timers, but this method made him so aware of time that unnecessary three-timer talks became rare.

Personal calls—twelve things you can do while you're on the phone

1. Clip torn-out newspaper articles.
2. Review tomorrow's schedule on your calendar.
3. Look through catalogs and tear out the pages you're interested in.
4. Pay bills, or write a check to your favorite charity.
5. Unpack groceries.
6. Update grocery and errands lists.
7. Put away things in the dish drainer or dishwasher.
8. Program your VCR.
9. Pull out ingredients for a casserole or salad.
10. Put some hand laundry in to soak.

11. Do your nails.
12. Sew on a button.

Keep a basket near your phone to toss in the small tasks that are convenient to do while on the phone.

For telephone convenience

- Use a shoulder attachment that frees your hands so you can take notes, cook, or do simple housecleaning chores.
- Keep extensions in the kitchen and work areas, and see that cords are long enough for ample mobility, or use a cordless phone.

10

Combating Procrastination and Perfectionism—and Finding Your Optimum Workstyle

Often it is the self-saboteurs that do in our plans for productivity and effective time management: procrastination, perfectionism, and a workstyle that goes against the grain. Here are some ideas to help you work *for,* not against yourself.

Procrastination and Perfectionism

Is procrastination at the root of many of your unfinished tasks? Have you labeled yourself a "hopeless procrastinator" and blamed yourself for your "psychological failing"?

You may be surprised to learn that while paralysis by procrastination does plague many people, often it is an organizational problem—not a psychological one. We practically set ourselves up to fail when we say things like "I'll clean up the workroom as soon as I finish this," or "Why bother starting? I'll never finish the whole thing anyway." Most people who procrastinate are overwhelmed by the way they *perceive* a task. The project seems "too big," the playroom "too messy." The best way to eliminate procrastination is to change your point of view and *divide larger tasks into smaller, more manageable ones.*

The Four Toughest Procrastination Problems and How to Solve Them

First problem: Knowing where to start

- Choose a starting action. Regardless of complexity, *all* projects can be broken down into various components, steps, or tasks. Brainstorm and list, in no special order, every task you anticipate needing to do for a project. Then pick one and begin.
- Is there a particular task you do regularly that is always a pain to begin? Routinize your opening moves. For example, I ease into the task of writing client reports by starting with a standard introduction: name, address, nature of consultation, etc. This routine moves me right into the heart of the task. *Or . . .*
- Make your first step a "baby step": Let's say you decided two weeks ago that your messy central desk drawer is no longer tenable, but you've been "too busy" to tackle it. Start to clean it out by picking up *one* paper clip and making a decision: do you want to throw it away, or put in a paper clip holder? Continue this process until the paper clip problem is solved, and then move on to rubber bands.
- Make it a group effort: When the situation allows, create a "team." Whether it's your colleague, a neighbor, or a friend, collaborating will energize you and force you to commit yourself. Managers who join forces to solve tough business problems and writers who review each other's work often find that being accountable to another person is motivating and often serves as a source of support.

Second problem: making big tasks manageable

- The chunk method: "Chunk" a big job down into its components. "Develop a new client presentation" can be chunked into: (1) Buy two books on sales, (2) List good sales ideas, (3) Compose a first draft, (4) Test draft on colleagues,

(5) Complete final version. Transfer one or two of these chunks from your Master List to your Daily List until the task is completed.

- Divide large tasks according to your available time. One entrepreneur produced documentation for a bank loan on alternate Sunday evenings between 6:00 P.M. and 8:00 P.M., her only "free" time.
- Try Alan Lakein's "Swiss cheese" technique. Punch holes into big projects by executing "instant tasks" that can be done in five minutes or less: Draw up a short outline for a report; list conference attendees; make one or two calls to get preliminary information.

Third problem: you just don't want to do it because it's boring or unpleasant

Strategy no. 1: Let someone else do it. Avoid the martyr's role by asking, "Is it more important that *I* do this job, or that it get done?" With that question in mind, consider your alternatives. You could:

- *Delegate.* Assign the project, or a piece of it, to a staffer. If you're a whiz at drafting proposals but not so great at editing and polishing, let someone who has those skills take over.
- *Hire an outside service.* Backlogged on correspondence? It may be well worth the investment to hire a temp for a few hours to help you catch up. If you are reluctant to spend the money, place a dollar value on *your* time and on the temp's time . . . and your concern will quickly disappear.
- *Barter.* Trade your detested task for a colleague's. One magazine editor writes headlines for a coworker, who takes on the proofreading job she hates.

Strategy no. 2: "Reward for punishment." Remember when you were a kid and you got a balloon from the dentist for being good? We may be grown up, but we still like to be rewarded for being put through the mill. Reward yourself in proportion to the completed task and your level of dislike.

- A fifteen-minute yoga break, or a walk to the park, can make up for twenty minutes of filing drudgery. Completing your taxes might rate a night on the town. Don't forget to check your daydream list (page 86) for ideas.
- Keep your work environment pleasant. Make the space around you comfortable—surround yourself with things that bring you pleasure: your child's painting, music, a favorite mug or souvenir.

Strategy no. 3: Distract yourself into action.

- Wear your Walkman and listen to music or a book-on-tape while doing the ironing and other tedious household chores.

Fourth problem: No immediate payoff

- Motivating yourself to start a project that won't come to fruition for weeks or months can be a drag. Try this technique: Build in mini-completions by establishing interim completion points. For example, get feedback on the first draft of a policy paper; publish one section of a longer report in the company newsletter.

Six more "anti-procrastination" techniques

1. Take a "legal" break. Set your timer for ten or fifteen minutes and do something pleasurable. Flip through a magazine, work a crossword puzzle. The trick to making this work is keeping the bargain you made with yourself and returning to the task when the alarm sounds.
2. Here's an offbeat idea: Do *nothing* for fifteen minutes. Force yourself to stare at the work you dread, forbidding yourself to tackle the materials. One lawyer who tried the technique said that "By that time, you're practically on fire to get started."
3. Use the "Well, as long as I . . ." technique: "Well, as long as I've got this file open, I'll organize it"; "Well, as long as this

paper is in my hand, I'll file it." You'll be amazed at how contagious this rationale is.

4. Do the piles of paper on your desk inspire you or terrify you? If you get paralyzed, make it a priority to clear your desk surface of everything except the task at hand.

5. Feel yourself slipping into debilitating inertia? Alan Lakein suggests sitting quietly with your eyes closed. Say to yourself, "Well, I'm not going to do it, but this is what I would do if I were going to do it." Working through the task imaginatively often gets your juices flowing and encourages you to act.

6. If you are vehemently resistant to a particular task, reevaluate it. Ask yourself what would happen if you didn't do it. Be honest. If you can live with the fallout, just cross it off your list.

Great galvanizers

- On the left side of a piece of paper, list the negatives of your procrastination. Note everything from "I hate the damn thing" to "I'll miss my deadline!" On the right, list the benefits and delights of completing the task—and you will soon see how the pros far outweigh the cons.

- Set the deadline for the task just before a holiday or the start of your vacation. You'll be surprised to find how this inspires you.

- Commit yourself to a "public" launch date. Intentionally backing yourself into a corner will spur you into action.

- Plan an event which will force you to take action. Six months after moving to a new office, the employees of one company were still stepping over unpacked cartons. A smart-thinking secretary suggested they have an office-warming party the following month, and lo and behold they were unpacked in record time.

Loosening the Vise of Perfectionism

Perfectionism is exhausting to contemplate, and it's not what good organizing is about. Good organizing has to do with making things "sufficient to the need" —while perfectionism is, by definition, "excessive to the need."

Perfectionism can lead to procrastination. One secretary complained that her boss never gets a letter out in fewer than three drafts, no matter how trivial the correspondence. Or it can lead to overkill. A young banker, when asked to put together some figures on U.S. trade with Norway, compiled a twenty-page report including not only the figures, but complex graphs and flow charts—when all that was required was a two-page summary. He was reprimanded for wasting time.

Ask yourself this question if you suspect perfectionism is rearing its ugly (albeit well-organized) head: "Is the amount of time and effort I'm putting into this task warranted by the potential payoff?"

If the answer is no, readjust your goals. Bring your efforts and the payoff into sync.

Finding Your Optimum Workstyle

Finding your own workstyle, rather than working against the grain, can give you a big boost in efficiency and can help alleviate procrastination tendencies. The following questions will help you identify your personal workstyle.

- *Do you prefer "hard-to-easy" or "easy-to-hard"?* Do you like to tackle the hardest parts of a big job first? Or do you prefer easing into a big task? Neither approach is "right," it's just got to be right for you. For those who prefer to ease in, it's important to make sure you don't avoid the tough stuff, which is usually the heart of the matter. Conversely, if you start with the more difficult tasks, don't forget to wrap up the loose ends.

- *Do you prefer working on a variety of tasks, or are you a one-project-at-a-time person?* One writer I know has learned she does best if she works on four different articles at one time rather than just one. She claims that the variety increases her efficiency, bypassing boredom. Her writing colleague, however, finds variety distracting and moves much more quickly concentrating on one assignment at a time.

  If you, too, are the variety type, remember to keep careful track of deadlines in your calendar as you bounce from project to project.

- *Do you know your tolerance levels?* While one person can concentrate productively for four hours straight, another can get fuzzy after an hour. Listen to your body signals. When you've read the same sentence three times, your neck is aching, and you no longer give a damn, it's time to quit. Pushing yourself beyond your tolerance limit is unproductive. Doubt it? Just compare the quality of work done when you're fresh and when you're tired.

- *Do you know your biorhythms?* As discussed on pages 93–94, tackle the toughest parts of a task during your peak performance time.

- *Do you work best in a pressure cooker or on a slow flame?* Pacing can be key to your productivity. Determine whether you work best by evenly pacing a task, lopping off a large chunk at the beginning, or cramming it all into the tail end. Some of us find that deadline pressure gives us an adrenaline high, while for others tight deadlines bring on anxiety attacks. Find your personal style and make the most of it.

11

Too Many Things to Do and Not Enough Time to Do Them?—A Cornucopia of Timesaving Tips

Time is precious—and more so now, it seems, than ever before. Wherever I go, one of the first questions I am asked is "How do I get it all done in twenty-four hours?" Believe it or not, you *can* get it all done if you follow the basic timesaving tips you will find in this chapter.

Power Packs—Getting the Most Out of Five Minutes

Double up

- Do small tasks simultaneously: Exercise while watching TV; sew on buttons while your twelve-year-old rehearses his lines for the class play. Sort mail or flip through catalogs while on the telephone. Polish silver while your clothes are in the dryer. Make up the bed while waiting for the coffee to brew.

Creative ways to use small bits of time

If you've ever dropped loose change into a piggy bank, you were probably astonished to find how quickly those coins added up to "real money." Think of time the same way. Each of us has small "coins" of time we spend waiting each day: for the elevator, at the doctor's office, in the bank line. You will be amazed to learn how much free time you can buy with this "small change" of time.

What you can do in five minutes

- Make an appointment
- Make out a party guest list
- Write or dictate a short note
- File your nails
- Water the plants

What you can do in ten minutes

- Pick out a birthday card
- Sort through the daily mail
- Order tickets for a concert or ball game
- Repot a plant
- Hand wash some clothes
- Take a catnap
- Scan a magazine article
- Dust the living room
- Straighten up your desk

What you can do in thirty minutes

- Skim a report and mark parts for further study
- Sort through backed-up journals, newspapers, and magazines
- Needlepoint, knit, or work on a craft
- Take a few bites out of a complex task

Making the most of "found time"

Found time is chunks of time that come up 'twixt and 'tween our regular activities. In many cases, you can anticipate and prepare to use found time efficiently and productively.

- *When going to an appointment.* Anticipate some waiting time during which you can update your expense accounts, write notes to clients, and update your to-do list. Your "traveling work kit" should include note paper, envelopes, stamps, pen, highlighter, calculator, Post-its, and 3" x 5" cards to jot notes on.
- *Waiting in line.* Organize your briefcase, do some discreet isometrics or breathing exercises, think about what you're going to wear tomorrow.
- *On the bus.* Make out your shopping list, add up your expense account, review a memo for a meeting, read trade journals or magazines.
- *While driving.* Put a language tape in your tape deck.
- *In the doctor's waiting room.* Outline a report, pay bills, write in your "daydream journal."
- *Between appointments.* Pick out a birthday card.

Take advantage of exercise time and walk time

- Many executives find that exercise or walking time gives them a great opportunity to organize their thoughts, think about their priorities, and develop strategies in a pressure-free environment.
- My friend Marsha gets through her morning regimen by listening to books-on-tape on her Walkman. She gets so absorbed that she not only "reads" more books, she loses track of how far she's walking.

Plan ahead

- Set out clothes and utensils the night before.
- Check beforehand that you have all the information you need to write your report.

Finding an Hour for Yourself

"Is there ever going to be any time for me?" As each of us goes through the day, we often assign a lesser priority to ourselves than to the people who claim our time. But not taking time for ourselves saps our energy and our ability to meet those demands to which we are committed. Carving out personal time is just as important as doing things for others. Here is a list of things you can do to create air pockets of "time for me" in your life.

- Delegate grocery shopping to an older child.
- *Don't* clean up your child's room—teach your child to do it. Painful as the first few times may be, it will be better for you both in the long run.
- Buy prepared foods or order dinner in once or twice a week.
- Choose one day—like a Sunday, when you have a block of time—and cook for the week. Then dinner becomes a matter of popping a cookbag in the microwave and making a salad.
- Let the answering machine pick up your calls for an hour every day.
- If you have kids, join co-op play groups and school-travel car pools. It'll save you tons of time driving to and from.
- Organize a family chore system.
- Use pickup and delivery services. Hire a high school or college student to run errands.
- Buy groceries in bulk to cut down on shopping trips.
- Keep up with reading by listening to tapes while walking, driving, and doing housework.

Eleven "Mini-vacation" Treats

With the time you've saved, give yourself a mini-vacation once or twice a week—a half hour or an hour of pure pleasure.

- Visit a museum.
- Read a novel or mystery story.
- Meet a friend for a drink.
- Take a dance class.
- Take a bubble bath.
- Get a massage.
- Have a picnic with your spouse and/or children.
- Call up a friend you haven't spoken to for a long time.
- Take a walk.
- Take a nap.
- Put your feet up and read a magazine.

Consolidate your efforts

- When doing a task, keep your movements "tight"—complete tasks in one geographical space before moving to another. Pull up the sheets, blanket, and spread on one side of the bed before crossing to the other. When cleaning the bathroom tub, clean the tiles around it before moving to the sink.

Instant-action chores

- Chores seem much less onerous if you don't put them off. Make the bed as soon as you get out of it. Do the dishes as soon as you finish the last bite.

Six ways to make routine errands easier

1. Designate a spot for all items needing repair or cleaning so you can grab them on your way out the door.
2. Hire an errands runner and an "everything" person. Many busy people I know have found that hiring a high school or college student to take care of their routine chores offers a *spectacular* timesaving benefit. Amanda, a working mom whose precious family weekend time was being consumed by tedious errands, hired Bernie, a local high school junior, to do many of them for her. The free time she gained was well worth the relatively small expense, and is one of the best bargains she ever made.
3. If you must do errands yourself, limit your errand running to once or twice a week. Save the trips to the dry cleaner and pharmacy for your grocery-shopping day.
4. Group your errands geographically. Ask yourself, "As long as I'm going to the pharmacy, what other tasks and errands can I knock off in that neighborhood?" Carry a small errands notebook with you and consult it to make sure you've done all you can.
5. Patronize stores that deliver. Many pharmacies, grocery stores, butcher shops, and dry cleaners will deliver either free or for a small charge.
6. Bank as much as possible by phone or computer.

Four tricks with timers

You can use your kitchen timer, or a watch with an alarm, as a handy reminder on many occasions.

1. It's easy to get so absorbed in a project that you forget to leave for an appointment. Let your timer be your guide.
2. Need to phone someone at eleven? Set your timer.
3. You've decided to devote an hour a day to straightening out your closet. Set your timer accordingly, packing it in when the alarm sounds. *Note:* You can expand this method and

use your timer to break your day down into specific "periods," like school periods, for specific tasks: correspondence, paying bills, cleaning the fridge.

4. Do you work at home and want to create more quality time with the kids? Organizer Ronni Eisenberg suggests setting your timer for fifteen-minute playtime sessions. Not only do you gain more time with your children, but they learn that when the timer goes off, it's back to work for you. Try tackling a project you and your child can complete within the fifteen-minute period—one corner of a jigsaw puzzle, say.

Three more timesavers

1. Before you take up a new hobby or pastime, evaluate your time realistically. Many people are really overextended, yet if we are not into aerobics, music lessons, and karate, we seem to feel we are not doing our civic duty. Before taking on a new activity, plan to drop one or two current activities that are no longer of interest to you.

2. Learn to budget time realistically. For seven days, time routine chores and get an accurate sense of how long a task really takes. Homemaker Mary Emrich said in *USA Today,* "One day I timed scrubbing the kitchen. It took thirty-five minutes. I've since timed all my routine chores. Doing so has helped me utilize my time better."

3. Use laborsaving devices or appliances as much as possible. Take advantage of easy-care materials, no-iron fabrics, self-cleaning ovens, and "no-show" carpets.

Up and Out and On Time

On being on time

Alec Mackenzie tells of a sign in a doctor's office that reads, "Don't be late, you're hurting three—yourself, the next in line, and me." Are you a latenik? Consider these suggestions.

- Don't do "just one more thing" or take "just one more call." When it's time to leave, go.
- Plan realistically. Traffic is *always* heavy at 9:00 A.M. and 5:00 P.M. Friday nights are *always* madness at the airport. So make sure to allow twice as much time as you think you need to get where you want to go.
- Use this time-honored trick: Set your watch, and all the clocks in your home, ten minutes ahead. Even though you *know* you're fooling yourself, seeing the lateness of the hour will get you going.

When *you* are the one left waiting

- Your best friend is always fifteen minutes late. Adjust yourself, and show up fifteen minutes late yourself—and steal a bit of time for something else. *Or* . . .
- If you can't bring yourself to be late, tuck a few articles or some work into your briefcase and turn your irritation into productive waiting time.

Meeting deadlines

- Set your own deadline a few days before the due date to give yourself a cushion. You may even enjoy the satisfaction of turning work in early.
- Stay on top of deadline dates. Occasionally they change, so it's wise to check back once or twice over the course of a long-term project to make sure the original deadline still holds.
- If your boss hits you with conflicting deadlines, ask him/her to set priorities. Simply say, "Since there's not enough time for me to complete both these tasks by this date, which should I do first?"

Rev Up Your A.M. Routine

Start your morning the night before

- Make your morning as automatic and decisionless as possible. Each night, select the outfit you'll be wearing the next day and iron if necessary. Remember to select jewelry, scarf, and any other accessories, and check whether shoes need buffing.
- Set up the coffee pot, set the table for breakfast, and take out the nonperishables you plan to eat.
- Fill juice glasses in the evening and then put them in the refrigerator. The frosty glass gives a nice early-morning lift.
- Use "night-before" checklist: Plan and lay out clothes, set the table for breakfast, pack up briefcases and school bags.

A.M. logistics

- For the sleepyheads in your house, here's a mean (but effective) trick: Put the alarm clock on the other side of the room so your late-risers will have to get up to turn it off.
- Avoid bathroom gridlock by staggering wake-up times whenever possible. *Hint:* Get your teens into (and out of) the bathroom first, or you may never get your turn.

Getting up and out stress-free

- Keep all the "stuff to go"—briefcases, backpacks, books—by the front door so that when it's time to leave, all your family has to do is grab and run.
- Theater tickets? Birthday cards and bills to mail? Keep them in a small basket on a table near your door so you'll be sure to pick them up on your way out. If you're a stubborn forgetter, put these items right in front of the door so you'll have to step over them to get out.
- For routine reminders, create a checklist and pin it to the door: phone machine on, oven off, lights out, cat out of the closet?

- For special reminders ("Have oil checked"), Post-it: on your door, dashboard, briefcase—wherever you're sure to see the note.

Too Much to Do? Do What You Do Best—Find Ways to Delegate the Rest

We are all familiar with the tremendous pressure to "do it all," the benefit of which is self-reliance, the detriment, stress and migraines. Other cultures have long known the value of cooperative effort as a means of sharing the workload, increasing productivity, and decreasing anxiety. There's a lesson to be learned from them.

Letting someone else do it—delegating—is the biggest timesaver of all. Do what you do best. Delegate, and eliminate the rest. Here are some creative, ingenious, low-cost ways to employ delegation in your daily life.

Barter

Bartering is a neat way of getting the services you need by trading off your own time and skills. This is particularly useful in unloading those tasks you detest. The key to bartering is identifying things you like doing and matching them up with other people's skills and preferences. For example:

- I organized an office of a client with a successful seminar business, and in exchange she developed a marketing program for me.
- Two secretaries in an insurance firm traded off this way: Ann handled all the filing drudgery, and Frances fielded customer inquiries and complaints.

Co-op and pool resources

- Carpooling, play groups, and baby-sitting pools are great time- and money-savers. Experiment. Can you co-op grocery shopping, waiting for deliveries, etc.?

Find that extra help when you need it

- Rely on specialists. Sometimes they provide more services than you realize. Journalist Jane O'Reilly said, "I once spent a week getting a vaccination certificate stamped. I wondered, does Elizabeth Taylor have to do this? No, and neither did I. The travel agent will get the tickets and see to the certificate, free of extra charge." There are many other experts who can guide you through some trouble spots: academic advisory services, tutors, etc. There are even services to help you straighten out health insurance and other claims so you can get what you are entitled to.
- As mentioned earlier, make use of pickup and delivery services offered by neighborhood merchants. And don't forget messenger services. Save time by letting them do your deliveries.
- One working mother opened a charge account with a taxi company. They chauffeured her children to their various appointments and also picked up and delivered laundry and packages.

In-your-home services

Today's two-paycheck, stressed-out families are finding that they can get almost any service they need at home, in hours that suit them, often for no more than it would cost outside. You may want to treat yourself to some of these services:

- Exercise trainers
- Manicurists and pedicurists
- Hairstylists
- Masseurs and masseuses
- Dog groomers and walkers
- Mobile boat and car repairmen
- People to clean your barbecue grill
- Tutors of math, physics, chemistry, languages
- Delivery of full meals, not only from your local pizza parlor, but from restaurants

- *Additional tip:* It may be more cost-effective to pay the premium to get the plumber in before 9:00 A.M. or after 6:00 rather than lose time at work.

If you can't find the services you want in the Yellow Pages, look for them in your local paper or pennysaver, or on the bulletin board at the supermarket. And always be sure to check references before allowing a stranger into your home.

Part Three

CLUTTER
AND
CLOSETS

12

The Clutter Crisis—
Eliminating Distressing Disarray

How do you know if you are in a clutter crisis? Easy.

- Are you tripping a lot?—that is, tripping over bottles that have to be recycled, overdue library books, unmarked VCR tapes, and your children's computer games?
- Are other people aware of clutter you no longer notice? I was visiting my cousin, who was working with me on this book, and to illustrate the clutter concept I pointed and said, "like those cartons next to the cabinet." She said, "What cartons?"
- Are you sharing your living room with an ever-encroaching pile of "stuff"?—skates, pictures for framing, leftover Christmas cards, screwdrivers . . . all of which have a purpose and a function—but not where they are.

Three basic rules are helpful in getting a grip on clutter.

1. Decide what's valuable to you and what isn't. Whatever comprises your clutter may be very useful, or it may be junk. But you might not be able to tell the difference, because you can't "see" it. When clutter has been hanging around for a while, it often takes on a life of its own. You might want to ask a friend or neighbor to help you objectify your clutter—decision making is the first step to a (reasonably) clutter-free future.

2. Bite the bullet. When you begin using the tips in this chapter, carry a big trash bag with you at all times and go into the project expecting from the outset that a good half of your clutter will hopefully wind up in the bag.

3. As a wise person once said, "A place for everything and everything in its place." Once your clutter is placed in its proper home, it's not clutter anymore.

Getting a grip on clutter not only will allow you to move toward organization, it will allow you to move comfortably and easily around your home.

Three Strategies for a (Reasonably) Clutter-free Future

Strategy no. 1. Keep your mess at bay: five easy clutterbusters

To reduce the occasion for things to be left around, make it effortless to put things away. Here are some ideas:

1. At each reading chair, create a "parking zone" for half-read books, magazines, or newspapers. A basket or magazine rack will do, or consider a pocket caddy (a cloth envelope with a long tongue fitted with snaps to attach to the chair underneath the cushion). It's also nice to have a small side table with a drawer for pens, pencils, etc.

2. Do you sew or knit while watching TV? Buffing shoes is a good TV-time activity, too. Keep your current project or buffing kit under a skirted chair.

3. Board games like Scrabble and Monopoly are fun to play, but they're a nuisance when they're left out. Keep a low cabinet in the family room for quick, easy put-away.

4. Cut down on kiddy clutter: Keep a drop basket in your family room for toys the kids have dragged in. Then, twice a week, empty the basket.

5. Here' a quick convenience tip: Keep a small can of furniture spray and some clean rags in a drawer in the living room for quick touch-ups.

Strategy no. 2. Move clutter from where it is to where it's supposed to be

- Keep a small wheeled cart in your family room and other main clutter areas so you can easily gather up napkins, glasses, and cracker boxes and return them to their rightful places in the kitchen.

- At the Kleins', the whole family likes to gather in mom and dad's bedroom to watch TV. By the end of the evening, there's quite a collection of glasses, candy wrappers, and soda cans. To quickly and conveniently alleviate the mess, the Kleins keep some colorful, nonbreakable serving trays in their bedroom. Before bedtime, the kids are assigned the job of carting all the leftovers and snack stuff to the kitchen.

- Are your kids and spouse deaf to your cries to pick up after themselves? Create a character ("I'm the Wicked Witch of the North") who periodically sweeps through the house with a laundry bag "clutternapping" the offending items. The captured stuff can be ransomed for a quarter, or it won't be returned for a week.

- If your house has two floors, keep objects going upstairs or downstairs in a basket near the steps, and pick them up as you travel.

- Keep a lost-and-found box in a central location for all those unmatched, odd items that turn up: jigsaw puzzle pieces, unmatched gloves, loose socks, etc. Go through the box once a week, and if you haven't found a home for those lost items in a few weeks, toss.

Strategy no. 3. Short-order room pick-up

Okay, let's face it. Clutterwise, your family room has gotten out of control. It's been invaded by last week's Sunday paper, a pile of mending, Timmy's Sega Genesis, one sneaker, those all-important instructions for the new VCR, and more. Here are three nifty ways —and one emergency plan—to get that room picked up in short order. Choose the method that works best for you.

- *The "junk chair."* Small piles of clutter all over the room can be paralyzing. It may be easier for you to cope with the mess if you consolidate all of it on one "junk chair," thereby clearing other surfaces. Then, piece by piece, start sorting things out and putting them away.
- *The "clock" technique.* Stand at the entrance to the room, designating that spot as twelve o'clock. Work the room systematically, clearing up the area at one o'clock, two o'clock, three o'clock, etc., till you return to your starting point. By the time your "clock" strikes twelve again, you're home free.
- *The "destination" technique.* Go around the room collecting things according to their destination. Load all kitchen stuff on your trolley and return it to the kitchen. Then start on all items that belong in the bedroom and follow suit for each new destination, one location at a time. *Do not* start washing the dishes or straightening the closet at this time. Stick to your picking-up project only, and leave the cleaning and organizing until later.
- *Emergency pick-up.* Your mother-in-law is at the door and the house is a disaster. Keep a "clutter depot" in each room —an attractive toy box, a large terra cotta planter, a wicker basket—and hide all the stuff in it temporarily. Don't forget to empty it when mama clears out.

The Seven-step Deep Clutter De-clutter Plan

Deep clutter is serious clutter. I'm not talking about the occasional sneaker left in the hall; I'm talking about the sneaker left in the hall, or kitchen, or den two months—or two years —ago.

But don't panic. No matter how old, clutter is simply a collection of individual *things* that can be put away, given away, or thrown away.

Dealing with deep clutter requires two things: determination and a solid de-clutter plan. You're obviously already determined, so here's the plan.

1. Set time bites. You don't need to take a deep breath and charge into the mess in one fell swoop. Setting unrealistic goals can be paralyzing. *Do not* plan to work more than half an hour a day on plowing through the piles. You're more likely to get the job done if you set regular "time bites"—every day if you can, but at least twice a week—and stick to them. Remember to mark your work sessions in your calendar.

2. Prepare. Get two cartons. Mark one "Giveaway" and the other "Goes elsewhere." Get a box of big plastic garbage bags for things you are going to toss.

3. Get started. Many people cry, "I don't know where to begin!" Start with something small and not intimidating—perhaps a small drawer in a living room table. If it *all* seems intimidating, stand in the middle of the room, close your eyes, turn around once, and point.

4. De-cluttering. You have committed yourself to working for half an hour, but set your timer for twenty minutes to allow yourself ten minutes for cleanup. Go to your first deep-clutter location (selected in Step 3), pick up the first item closest at hand, and follow these easy instructions.

- *Decide whether to keep it, toss it, or give it away.* See page 137 for more detail on how to decide what to keep and what to throw away.
- *Put it in the right place.* A "keep" goes in the "Goes elsewhere" carton, a "toss" in the garbage bag, and something with wear left in it (that you no longer care about) in the "Giveaway" carton.
- *Keep going.* Pick up the next-closest item, and do the same.
- *Note "things to do."* Some items will call for action: hanging a picture, taking the ice skates in for repair. Mark the task in your to-do list and put the items in a visible corner.

5. Wrap-up. When the timer goes off, that's your signal that you have ten minutes left. This is the time to distribute items from your "Goes elsewhere" carton to where they belong:

those sneakers belong in your child's closet, the bills belong on the desk, books in the bookcase, etc. *Very important: Do not* try to organize your child's closet or the bookcase at this time. That's another project for another day. Just return the items to their appropriate places as best you can.

6. *Start again tomorrow.* Start tomorrow where you left off and keep moving, first around the periphery of the room, and then in toward the center.

7. *Take care of loose ends weekly.* Once a week, give away your giveaways, and take care of those to-do items: bring those ice skates into the repair shop, and hang that picture.

Two hints to make de-cluttering less stressful

1. *Call a clutter buddy.* If you have trouble making decisions about what to keep and what to toss, ask a friend to stand by and be your conscience. Some people I know who are inveterate clutterers formed a support group of like-minded friends to support each other and share progress.

2. *Record your progress.* Some people find that recording what they have accomplished that day—"Cleared out right drawer of coffee table"—in a notebook spurs them on and gives them a real sense of achievement.

And once you've de-cluttered? Just follow the clutter maintenance strategies outlined on pages 128–130 to keep everything in its appropriate home.

Hanging On to the Little Losables and Other Convenience Tips

Here's how to keep track of those odds and ends that can drive you nuts.

Keeping keys under control

- Ever misplace your house keys? When you walk in the door, drop them into a little bowl or tray right by the entrance. Or, hang the keys on a hook or nail.

- If you carry a lot of keys, label them to avoid confusion. Scotch tape a tiny slip of paper with an abbreviation—"BD" for back door, say—onto the key. You can also distinguish your most important keys with a dot of nail polish.
- Set up a family key rack so everyone has easy access to the storage room, garage, etc. A wooden plaque with rows of nails, each labeled with the appropriate key, might actually encourage your kids to keep their skateboards, basketballs, etc., in the garage instead of the family room.
- Tag those little keys that come with suitcases and briefcases with small stringed tags that you can purchase at a stationery store.
- Have you accumulated a collection of mystery keys? It's safer to keep them than to toss them out. Store them in an envelope for a day you might need them.
- Losing the combination to a lock can be a major headache. Make a list of all combinations—your bicycle locks, your locker at the fitness center—and keep it in a place accessible only to you and your family.

Have coins where you need them for when you need them

Isn't it fun to sit in the exact change lane at a tollbooth behind a person who can't find exact change? Isn't it even more aggravating when that person is you? My trick to avoid getting caught short is to dump out all the coins I've accumulated by the end of the day and allocate them.

- *For the car:* Keep a taxi driver's coin dispenser on the dashboard, or a coin holder on a flat surface you can easily reach.
- *For the bus:* Keep a small coin purse in your wallet.
- *For the coin laundry:* Keep a jar of coins near your laundry products to keep them handy.

Useful Home Diagrams

- Ever stare helplessly in the dark at your electric circuit breaker or fuse box? Label the switches (and keep a flashlight handy) and as a useful backup make a drawing of the unit indicating which switch powers what and tape to the door of the fuse box for handy reference.
- In your workroom, outline hammer, saw, and other tools while they're on the wall (or on pegboard) so you know exactly where they belong. In the kitchen, outline the shapes of hanging pots and pans à la Julia Child.

More convenience tips

- Keep claim checks for shoe repairs, the dry cleaner, etc., handy in your wallet so you can pick the items up at your convenience.
- Use a bright-colored or textured wallet and avoid fishing in your bag.
- Do pens, pencils, scissors, and paper clips seem to get eaten up? Set up "supply depots" around the house. Also, keep stashes of note paper and blank pads in strategic locations —near telephones, and elsewhere—so you can jot a quick note or capture an idea.
- To avoid overlooking those little to-do's before you leave the house, pin a checklist to the front door that includes things like "Lights out?" "Thermostat down?" "Oven off?"

13

Storing Stuff

C an't find a thing? Are your closets and storage cabinets jammed with everything from puzzles and tablecloths to tinsel and poker chips? Take heart. Together we will find ways to store this . . . stuff . . . creatively. (Clothes closets are a different animal, and therefore warrant their own chapter. See Chapter 14 for tips on clothes and accessories.)

The majority of storage problems fall into one of three categories:

Overstuffing. In many cases, overcrowding is the result of poorly organized space rather than insufficient space.

Disorganization. You know it's in there, you just can't find it.

Insufficient space. You *really* don't have enough space. You need to create new storage opportunities.

Let's start by clearing out your closets.

Closets, Cupboards, and Cabinets

Your Step-by-Step "One Closet at a Time" Program

Clearing out a cabinet or storage area has much in common with clearing out a cluttered room, so some of the same steps are used for both.

Step 1: Select working times. Plan on working no more than a half hour a day—every day if you can, but at least twice a week. Set your timer to go off after twenty minutes, leaving ten minutes for closing out the day's work. Remember to mark your work sessions in your calendar.

Step 2: Prepare. Label two cartons "Giveaway" and "Store elsewhere." Have plenty of trash bags on hand for things you're going to toss. Get peel-off stickers big enough for you to write on.

Step 3: Work on one section at a time. Avoid *the* key closet-organizing error: pulling everything out onto the floor, then asking, "Why did I ever start this?" This usually leads to shoveling it all back in and slamming the door, leaving the closet in worse condition than when you started.

Instead: Select a finite work space—say, the lower left shelf of the hall closet. Ignore the rest until you get to it.

Step 4: Decide what to keep and what to throw away. See "But it might come in handy someday!" on page 137 for guidance on this often-difficult choice.

Step 5: Put the object in the right place. Is it going to stay in the present closet? Then put it back. Don't worry about "organizing" it just now. Something that belongs in another location goes in the "Store elsewhere" carton, a "toss" goes in the garbage bag, and something with some wear left in it goes in the "Giveaway" carton. Put stickers on the "store elsewheres" indicating where they go.

Step 6: Close out for the day. When the timer goes off, that's the signal that you have ten minutes left. Distribute the "store elsewheres" where they belong—the sports equipment to the front closet, etc. *Do not* at this time try to organize the area the item is going *to*. That's another project for another day. Push the Giveaway box to an unobtrusive location, enter any tasks ("Rewire the lamp") on your to-do list, and put those items in a corner. You are done for the day.

Step 7: Take care of business. Once a week, take your giveaways in to the thrift shop, and handle the to-do's.

Step 8: When the closet has been sorted out. Now it's time to consider the most effective and creative uses for the closet.

"But it might come in handy someday!"

The *most difficult part of organizing space is deciding what to keep and what to get rid of. This three-question "to keep or not to keep" test will help clarify your thinking.*

1. Have I used this item in the last year? If the answer is yes, keep it. If the answer is no, go to question #2.
2. Does this item have special meaning or value to me? Sentimental or esthetic value are perfectly legitimate reasons to keep the tassel from your graduation cap, or a beautiful seashell from your trip to Cape Cod. But if the answer is no, go to question #3.
3. Might this item come in handy someday? Aha! There's your Catch-22—*because there isn't anything in the world that might not come in handy someday.* If your answers to questions 1 and 2 were no, that's your cue to discard the item or give it away. (Make an appointment with yourself to donate these items to the local thrift shop and get a nice tax deduction.)

   Should the unlikely day ever come that you could have used that extra whatsis, the benefit in freeing up your storage space more than compensates for having to buy a new one.

Holding areas and other alternatives

When panic sets in at the thought of getting rid of things, here are some useful ideas for making the discarding process easier.

- Give yourself a transition period. Put those items you know should go but you can't let go of into a box. Set a toss-out date for three months from now. Then, if you haven't gone back to retrieve something from the box in that time, toss it. Even better: If you can't trust yourself, enlist a friend. One client of mine gave her box to a friend and instructed her to toss it if she hadn't requested it back in three months.

- For the real toughies, lease them your spare space—an extra closet or storage area—for a year. At the end of the year, evict them.
- Set up a grab bag. One man I know keeps a box of "get-riddable" things by the front door. He tells guests to check through it and see if there's anything they need. He not only gets rid of these things, he's become a real popular guy.

How to Solve Tough Storage Problems

Keeping your closets and storage areas in order is simple once you know the four basic principles of storing:

1. **Keep frequently used objects low and accessible.** Store less-used items on higher shelves or out of the way.
2. **Group like with like.** Keep sporting goods with sporting goods, blankets with blankets, bowls with bowls.
3. **Keep stacks small.** As a rule of thumb, stack no more than three items on top of each other. Stacking four mixing bowls is not only precarious, but it makes the first one too hard to retrieve.
4. **Maintain "fingertip storage" for items needed at a moment's notice.**

- Keep a first-aid kit in the kitchen where you're most apt to cut yourself; a can of spray cleaner and clean rags in a living room drawer for quick touch-ups.
- Store your vacuum cleaner in or near your living room area, where you are most likely to start vacuuming, instead of in a kitchen storage area.
- Store items you grab on your way out the door—umbrellas, tennis rackets, etc.—in a closet or rack near the door.
- Keep the file folders you use most often at hand in rolling carts or mobile caddies.

Our basic objective is to achieve convenience, as expressed by Alexandra Stoddard in *Style for Living: How to Make Where*

You Live You: "The more your organization is integrated into your every day, the more it will free your time."

Outside the Closet— Finding Storage Opportunities throughout Your Home

Insufficient closet space? You can create space-making alternatives almost anywhere in your home. Here's how:

Hang it

The most generous storage areas you have in your home are your walls and ceilings. Hanging not only expands your storage potential, but things become easier to find.

- Individual hooks on the wall or back of the door are helpful if you have only a few pieces to hang.
- Garage a mess? Hang big things like shovels, rakes, and ladders on the wall.
- Consider hanging pieces you don't usually consider "hangable." For example, a bicycle can be supported on the wall with spikes. Strollers can be hung too.
- Open rafters? Lining up skis across ceiling beams is a great way to store them for the summer.

Shelve it

Once you start thinking, you'll find lots of opportunities for creating new storage areas by installing shelves. Here are some shelf ideas:

1. Store items of approximately the same height on the same shelves. To set shelf height, measure a few typical items and allow a few inches above that.
2. Fixed shelves too high? Consider inserting a shelf, or hang an under-the-shelf rack from the shelf above.
3. And here are some more shelf ideas:

- Fill out a wall indentation with shelves. A five-inch-deep indent in a little girl's bedroom wall can be shelved and lined with dolls.
- Look for gaps to fill. My Aunt Shirley and Uncle Lou found a five-inch-wide gap in their kitchen, between refrigerator and range, which they shelved to create extra space for canned and packaged goods.
- Build new shelves on *any* vertical surface—for example, the back panel of a freestanding bookcase.
- Fit a window with a shelf unit for plants.

Contain it—inside or underneath

Decorative bowls and vases. One client stored small household items—glue, scissors, string—in an earthenware bowl placed on a shelf high enough so the doodads weren't visible.
Baskets. These are handy for linens, rolled-up towels, newspapers and magazines, board games.
Under the bed. Gain yards of space for seasonal or seldom-used belongings. Buy under-bed storage boxes for blankets and pillows, summer wear in winter, and even holiday decorations. Keep a list in your night table of what's in each under-bed box.
Under furniture. Put a skirt on your vanity table and tuck away the tote bag that has been standing in the corner of the room. My cousin, who collects makeup, stores her lipsticks in a box under her skirted vanity table.
Create new "furniture" out of storage. A writer who keeps old article files in two sturdy cardboard file boxes stacked them, tossed a pretty throw on top, added a lamp, and created a new end table.

Look for storage niches

- Spaces between objects offer hidden storage potential. Fit your folding stepladder in the small gap between washing machine and sink. What about a rack to hold newspapers or garbage bags? The space between an open door and the wall might be perfect for a fold-up drying rack, ironing board, or folding chairs.

Where to put those pesky odds and ends

- Keep umbrellas in several locations: near the door at home, on a hook at the office, and in your tote bag. That way you'll never get wet!
- Use containers designed for other purposes—for example, the compartments of a fishing tackle box are super for nails, small garden tools, jewelry, cosmetics, sewing or crafts supplies.
- Keep all gift wrap supplies—paper, scissors, ribbon, tape, tags, and shipping supplies—in one "wrapping center" box or carton. You'll save a lot of time and frustration hunting around for the scissors or tape.
- Clear kitchen canisters are nifty for small soaps, outsize paper clips, cotton pads.
- Are your extension cords all tangled up in a pile? Mary Ellen suggests winding each cord loosely and slipping it into a cardboard tube from paper towels or toilet tissue.
- Purchase "organizers"—bins, racks, baskets—at hardware or home stores. Decide what you'll be storing in each organizer before you buy; remember, if you don't plan, organizers just give you more space to be disorganized in.

Alternative spaces

As with containers, you can use storage space in unexpected ways.

- Linen closets make great storage closets for children's toys. They're easily accessible, and it's even handier to keep your sheets in the bedrooms where they're used.
- Tuck electronic components (stereo, TV, etc.) inside an antique cupboard or an armoire.
- Extra bookshelves can be home for your Walkman, tape recorder, or small electric fan. Curtain the space if you'd like, or put up an attractive screen.

"Divide and conquer"—create new storage space

- Many rooms can be partitioned into hidden storage areas by an attractive screen or curtain. One of my clients created a new storeroom by hanging a floor-to-ceiling drape across her long, narrow living room. Not only did she create valuable storage space, but she also benefited by making the proportions of the room more attractive.
- Make better use of corners. Use the screen and curtain idea to section off a corner of the room to hide caddies of cleaning supplies, games, and boxes of off-season clothes.
- Use the space between the window drape and wall for storing long, narrow objects—a small stepladder, etc.

Retrieving stored items

- If items are stored in a number of areas, list the locations and file the list in your "household" folder.

Books, Recordings, Films, and Videos

Books

Organizing your bookcase

- *Nonfiction:* Group the books by subject matter—biography, history, health, gardening, public affairs. Then, within each category, alphabetize by author.
- *Fiction:* Alphabetize by authors' last names.
- *Art books and other outsize books:* Set up a special high shelf. You might want to organize art books by period and/or by artist.
- *Cookbooks:* Set up a cookbook shelf in the kitchen. My sister, a dedicated cook, uses an available shelf in one of her kitchen cabinets.

- *An extensive library?* Apply label tapes (punched with a hand-held device available at stationery stores) to bookshelves to identify sections of your collection.

Too many books?

When the books start overflowing, it's time to sort through your collection and pull out duplicates, or books you're no longer interested in, and find them a new home.

- Donate your excess books to a library, school, or hospital. My friend Marsha used colored peel-off stickers to identify each book she wanted to give away. Then each week she pulled out as many giveaway books as a shopping bag would hold, and dropped the bag off at the local library.
- Consider a "book swap" party. A fun way to get rid of unwanted books is to ask your friends to bring over their unwanted books and hold a "book swap" where each person takes the books they want.

Extending bookshelf space

- Get a freestanding bookcase and put it against the wall or, if practical, make it a room divider. If you already have a bookcase room divider, stand another bookcase back-to-back with the first one.
- Assemble stackable plastic or wooden cubes and create a wall unit or room divider.
- Too many high shelves and not enough high books? Install an in-between shelf. Measure the space carefully to make sure the shelf is high enough for two rows of books. Allow about an inch for the shelf itself.
- Stand paperbacks in front-and-back rows. Reserve your favorites for the front row, and loosely pack the front row to make the back row accessible.
- As a general rule, keep books upright; don't stack them on their sides. It may seem like side-stacking saves space, but in doing so, you have effectively buried the bottom books.

Records, CDs, and Cassettes

Organizing records, CDs, and audiocassettes

Whether your music collection consists of CDs and audiocassettes, or you still relish your old LPs, these basic tips apply to all. Be sure to keep cassettes, records, and CDs separate.

- *Pop music:* Alphabetize by performer or band.
- *Classical music:* Organize alphabetically by composer. When an album features more than one composer, file by the composer you're most apt to remember.
- *Opera:* Most opera lovers prefer to alphabetize by the name of the opera rather than the composer (except maybe for true Wagnerians). Alphabetize albums featuring specific artists by singer. Here's a neat tip: Pull the librettos from albums and file them alphabetically into your bookcase, so they're readily available when you want to follow an opera on radio or television.

Storing records, CDs, and cassettes

- As an alternative to purchasing specially designed shelves and racks, improvise. One woman I know keeps cassettes in a wooden gift box that came with a bottle of wine; another uses shoe boxes covered with contact paper for CDs.
- Color-code your music. One music lover stores classical music in white units and jazz recordings in blue for at-a-glance ease and retrieval.
- Spare bookshelf space? Store music there and label the shelves or insert dividers between the different categories.

For the serious collector

- Set up a thorough catalog of your holdings on index cards or in your computer. Identify by performer or composer or opera, and cross-reference other elements of interest.

Films and Videotapes

Organizing films and videotapes

Films. Generally, I recommend organizing movie tapes alphabetically by title. If you have an extensive collection, however, consider organizing first by category—musicals, mysteries, Westerns—and then, alphabetically within the category.
Home videos. There are three methods I recommend:

- *Chronological.* File tapes by date. Be sure to label each tape at once, or you'll quickly be lost.
- *By event.* File under "Thanksgivings," "Christmases," "vacations," etc. (Don't forget to add the date on your label.)
- *By person.* When Norma videocams her kids, she uses a special tape for each child. She uses the "Katrina tape" for Katrina's first-grade show, and "Alicia's tape" for Alicia's birthday party. These make great gifts for your kids when they're grown.

Blank tapes. Always keep several blank tapes on hand to record TV shows or movies that you intend to watch once. Then record over them. Label them temporarily with peel-off stickers or Post-its.

Moving—Eight Steps to Get Where You're Going

Moving to a new location is always nerve-racking, but there are ways to move efficiently, and there's a bright side—you get to start fresh and hopefully solve some of your old storage problems.

If you choose to follow this eight-step method, you'll have to organize the packing yourself; it's too elaborate a project for most moving companies—but the benefits are substantial.

(Continued)

1. Prepare. Start accumulating large moving cartons at least several weeks in advance of the move. Liquor stores are a great source for strong, midsized boxes.
2. Pull out and sort the contents of your present closets and cabinets into broad categories: toys, linens, etc.
3. Dispose of giveaways and throwaways (review ideas on pages 136–138).
4. Make a plan of closets and storage areas in your new home and decide in advance which category of items will be stored in which closet or cabinet. Number closets and cabinets to identify them.
5. Decide on and implement if possible any necessary physical adjustments you will need to make to move in comfortably—i.e., put up new bookshelves, install pegboard or grids.
6. When packing, number each carton with the appropriate closet or cabinet number.
7. Direct the movers to which rooms which cartons go in.
8. Unpack the cartons into the appropriate closets in your new home.

And here's a moving tip from organizer Lucy Hedrick: Photograph your old closet before you tear it apart to record how you stored the contents, and make quick work of re-creating the closet in your new home. This tip also applies to a home renovation or redecoration.

14

The Organized
Clothes Closet

It is a well-known fact that clothes and accessories, no matter how stylish or expensive, become clutter when disorganized. How often have you searched frantically through your closet for your favorite blouse? And, when you finally found it, it was wrinkled beyond wearability because it was stuffed next to who knows what. Closet clutter generally breaks down into three problem areas:

1. Too many, too much—you don't wear them, but you can't part with them, either.
2. You wear them when you can find them, but half the time you can't find them.
3. You wear them, you need them, but you are running out of space.

This chapter will help you get closet-smart.

The Organized Clothes Closet—
How to Make It Happen

What to do with too much stuff

A change in season is a good time to review your closet and eliminate what you don't really use. In the fall, when you put away your summer clothes, cull the garments that won't be used again, and vice versa in the spring.

Easy choices: Get rid of garments that don't fit anymore, or damaged garments that aren't worth repairing.

Hard choices: Many people keep clothes they rarely wear and probably never will again, because who knows . . . the Nehru suit may yet live again. They simply can't stand to discard something that might someday be of some use. To gain a more objective focus, go through each item one by one and give it the "to keep" test. Ask yourself:

1. Have I used this item in the past year?
2. If not, do I love it anyway?

If you answer no to both questions, donate the item to your local thrift shop or the Salvation Army, or consider a resale consignment store to make back some of your investment.

Storing out-of-season clothes

- Infrequently used suitcases work best for storing out-of-season clothes. Old trunks are specially handy for bulky sweaters and blankets.
- Do you have some closet shelves too high up for regular use? They're fine for out-of-season storage.
- Pack seasonal ware in under-bed storage units. You can purchase them in department store closet shops.
- Here's a neat storage idea from Mary Ellen: If you've got a basement, store out-of-season clothes in large plastic trash cans with lids. Not only will your clothes be mothproof, they will be out of the way and stay dry in damp basements.
- If you store off-season wear out of sight, make a list of where your garments are stored and slip it into your "Household" folder.

Organizing your clothes

By type. First, hang similar articles together—sweaters with sweaters, shirts with shirts. Then sort your closet into four simple categories.

For the top half of the body:	Sweaters
	Light jackets
	Blazers
	Blouses
	Shirts
For the bottom half of the body:	Slacks
	Jeans
	Skirts
For the whole body:	Dresses
	Men's suits
Special-occasion wear:	Long dresses
	Party clothes

You may have noticed that there is no category for women's suits. I recommend hanging suit jackets with other jackets, and suit skirts with the rest of your skirts. This liberates these garments for their mix-and-match potential.

By use. Then within these categories, roughly sort into business clothes, casual, sportswear, and dressy.

Helpful hanger hints

- Garment bags are awkward and take up valuable space. I recommend them only for fragile clothing like lace or chiffon. The closet itself protects clothing from ordinary dust, and a dry cleaner's plastic bag offers extra protection if desired.
- Multiple skirt hangers are space savers, but having wrestled with a few myself, I prefer giving up that space and the aggravation with it. But if they work for you, by all means, use them.
- Empty hangers, particularly bent ones, take up valuable closet space. Sort through them periodically, toss the bent ones, and keep only the minimum you need in your closet. Store extras in a basket on the floor of your linen closet.

Coat closet boosters

- Keep only the current season's coats and jackets in the coat closet. Store next season's outerwear elsewhere. Buy an inexpensive freestanding wooden storage closet for your basement or attic, or under-bed storage boxes.
- A coat rack, either the old-fashioned freestanding kind or a handsome wall rack, is also a good supplement to the closet. Some people use them to keep everyday coats, hats, and bags handy. A coat rack is also more convenient for guests' coats than a coat closet. An umbrella rack or stand near the door can also be useful.
- To hang out wet coats, lay a strip of indoor-outdoor carpeting underneath a wall rack by the front door.
- If there's no light fixture in the closet, tie a flashlight to a hook.

Space-Stretchers

Get more mileage from the closets you've got

- If your closet is deep, install a parallel second rod to double the hanging space. Put clothing combinations worn most often in the front, and clothing worn less often in the back.
- If your closet ceiling is high, make more room for separates by installing two layers of hanging rods, the upper one for jackets and tops, the lower one for skirts and slacks. Designate a full-length area for dresses and longer items. Install shelves for luggage and seldom-used items in extra-high closets.

- In a normal-sized closet, you can make space by *lowering* the closet rod to make room for an extra shelf above. This works especially well for men's suits or if you don't wear dresses and don't need a full-length area.
- Carefully measure the closet's dimensions and insert a free-standing cabinet, either with open shelves or fitted with drawers.
- Add hooks to the side or on the back of the door for bathrobes and the nightgown you're currently wearing.
- Hang pants on slender towel racks installed on the back of the door.
- Place "special occasion" items—like party shoes and evening bags—in the harder-to-reach spots in your closet. Store in clear plastic bags or boxes, or label shoe boxes.

Create new space outside the closet

- A freestanding wardrobe or armoire can be used as an additional closet—in your bedroom for daily use, or elsewhere for off-season wear or overflow.
- Install hanging rods *outside* your closets. Do you have an underutilized alcove? Install a high rod for blouses, shirts, and jackets, leaving room for a dresser or desk below. Hide it from view with an attractive curtain.
- Buy a freestanding clothes rack (the kind you see in stores) and hide it with a decorative screen.
- If drawer space is generous and closets are limited, use drawers in unusual ways. One client folded her slacks in drawers. She "stagger-stacked" them, with the edge of each pair showing—like cards laid out for solitaire—making them easily visible.
- Turn bookcases into clothing shelves for sweaters and other foldables.
- Consider stackable plastic or wooden storage cubes for holding T-shirts, jeans, mufflers, etc.

Planning Your Wardrobe

"My closet is full and I don't have a thing to wear"

Planning your wardrobe will save you time, money, and aggravation. Many people tend to buy pieces on impulse without thinking of their overall wardrobe scheme, and then find that "must have" pink blouse stands alone and unused in their closet. These tips will give you a framework for your clothing selections.

- Go for mix-and-match versatility. Make sure you have at least two or three sweaters/blouses to wear with that paisley skirt.
- Be more creative in identifying clothing combinations. Punch a hole through an index card listing the garments that each piece of clothing can be matched with, and slip it over the hanger. You'll find this method expands your "outfit" potential in ways you may never have thought of—all without buying new clothes.
- If, on the other hand, you're a person who likes to get up and out with a minimum of clothing choices, pre-coordinate your three or four favorite outfits. Hang sweater, skirt, and blazer on one hanger, and you're off. Streamline travel by using the same method for outfits you will know you want to pack.

Organizing your shopping trips

- Try to buy "by outfit." Purchase the dress, shoes, stockings, bag, and accessories at one time so you're sure the outfit works. Cut down on impulse buying by making a shopping list of planned purchases.
- Many people find it convenient to do two big wardrobe shoppings a year. To make these productive, make up a list of the outfits and garments you think you need, keeping in mind your lifestyle and upcoming special events.
- On a high-powered schedule? Many department stores offer personal shopping services to help you coordinate your

wardrobe. Call ahead for an appointment, and give the shopper your size, your price range, and the kind of clothes you're looking for so she'll have a selection waiting for you when you arrive.

- If you need to buy things to match with something you already have, snip fabric from the inner seam of the garment. Tape it to a small index card and carry it with you so you can find perfect matchups when shopping. (Be sure to compare the colors in natural light.)

- After you buy a new article of clothing, use that "shopping high" to get rid of that old iffy garment you've been mulling over tossing. Yes, the miniskirt did come back. But (a) the look is different, and (b) *we* are different.

Accessories

It's 7:30 P.M., and you're late for your boss's retirement party. At the last minute you realize what your outfit is missing—that long gold necklace you got for Christmas. You go to your jewelry box and there it is, glinting from the tangled web of gold, silver, and coral chains. Only the rescue squad could untangle all that metal. You leave unadorned.

Sound familiar? Most of us have been there. Similar scenarios can be drawn for belts, scarves, gloves, hats, and even shoes ("where *is* that left shoe?").

Because of the varying sizes and shapes of accessories, we have to be innovative in making accessory space work. These suggestions can help.

Avoid tangled chains and necklaces

- Hang chains from a man's tie rack—no more than two or three on a hook.
- Hang necklaces from small hooks or nails inserted on the back of the closet door, or from hooks attached to pegboard or a grid. Or, as an alternative, insert cup hooks into the bottom of a wooden hanger, along the arms of a wooden

coat rack, inside your closet door, or to the bottom of a shelf.

- Here's a clever idea: Glue corkboard inside a picture frame, and hang necklaces and bracelets from pushpins. This is a simple and inexpensive technique, and it looks quite handsome.

Four more things you can do with jewelry

- Store jewelry in drawer dividers or small boxes in your dresser.
- Keep a decorative tray or dish on your dresser for rings and other items you wear every day.
- Large earring collection? Plastic ice-cube trays are great earrings holders—store one pair per cube.
- Here's a neat idea for pins: Rather than dumping them in a box, pin them to a T-shirt on a hanger. One woman attached her pins to her bedroom curtains and created a new look in window fashion.

Seven no-fail tips for belts, scarves, hats, and handbags

- For foolproof organization of ties or scarves, use three tie racks: one for solids, one for stripes, and one for prints.
- For handbags and belts, a large S-shaped hook placed on the clothes rod is a neat solution.
- A clear plastic shoe bag on the back of your closet door makes underwear, stockings, gloves, or socks easily visible.
- Hang scarves on slim metal towel racks attached to the back of the closet door.
- Tiered wire baskets also work well for socks and stockings.
- Store handbags upright on closet shelves in plate racks.
- Hats can be stacked conveniently on closet shelves, but I recommend you stack no more than three on top of each other—if possible, grouping the same type, such as fedoras, together. To keep lint-free, wrap in plastic dry-cleaner bags. Some people also hang hats as decorations.

Frequently Asked Questions

No matter how badly we want to get—and stay—organized, many of us are creatures of clutter. Here are some often-asked questions and answers about how to stay clutter-free when you're inclined not to.

Q: I'm hopeless. When I'm in a hurry I throw my clothes everywhere. Help!
A: I sympathize. I solved my own clothes clutter problem by designating a junk chair. Whenever I'm in a tossing mood I pile up stuff on that one chair *and nowhere else.* This confines the mess to one place, and makes putting away easier. And *do* put everything away at least every two or three days.

Q: When I trek home piled high with clothes from the dry cleaner's or from the store, I'm tired and in no mood to put things away. What do you suggest?
A: Put a hook on the bedroom wall to temporarily hang up dry cleaning. Let dry-cleaned clothes air out for a day before putting them away. Ideally, new clothes should be hung up immediately, but if you're really zonked, leave your packages on the junk chair, and get to them ASAP.

Q: My closet's sliding doors only open halfway, so half the closet is always blocked.
A: Divide clothes in the two halves of the closet by type—businesswear on one side, sportswear on the other. If you ever have an opportunity to redo your closet, exchange the sliding doors for the open-and-shut variety. They are much more convenient, and offer lots of back-of-the-door storage space.

Five tips for storing shoes and boots

- You can purchase special hangers fitted with pockets for shoes. Just be sure to check that the plastic pockets are sturdy. The disadvantage is that these hangers take up a lot of space.
- Create a floor shelf in your clothes closet to store winter boots, shoes, and skates.
- Get a shoe rack for the closet floor if you don't have room for the hanging variety. It keeps the shoes in order and will inhibit you from just tossing them into the closet.

Finishing touches

- You're dressing and oops—off pops a button. Keep a small sewing kit in your dressing area for quick patch-ups. The kit should include a small scissors to clip loose threads from clothing.
- Keep a lint remover in the closet or dressing area to take care of lint, pet hairs, etc.
- To extend the life of your buttons, Mary Ellen suggests sealing the threads by dotting the center of each button, front and back, with clear nail polish.

Part Four

HOMESTYLES
AND
LIFESTYLES

15

Recipe for an Organized Kitchen

Perhaps more than any other room in the home, the kitchen has a mystique all its own: Not only do we eat there, but we gather there to talk, about everything from the day's events to foreign policy. We write letters, we have fights, we do homework—all the while preparing, cooking, and serving food.

In many homes, the kitchen is the physical and emotional nerve center of the family. Thus it requires careful organization to ensure that it is efficiently and comfortably used.

In this chapter you will learn how to use your kitchen space more efficiently, find and create precious storage space, and make easy work of grocery shopping, menu planning, and food preparation.

Making Your Kitchen Space Work

Long marches between range, counter, and refrigerator can turn the production of the simplest meal into a marathon. According to Mimi Sheraton, former food editor of *The New York Times,* "the actual work area that includes range, sink and refrigerator should be small, so that those three major pieces of equipment are each no more than a step or pivot apart."

Though your kitchen may not be ideally designed, here are some ways to make it fuss-free.

Counters

A major problem for many people is freeing up enough counter space to lay out ingredients, cut, mix, and comfortably prepare foods. Here are some ideas.

Open up counter space

- Install a small wall shelf to hold canisters and those coffee cans and salt and pepper shakers now taking up valuable counter space.
- Consider small under-cabinet appliances. Some companies offer lines of small appliances, like toasters, which are designed to be installed between cabinet and counter.
- When was the last time you used that popcorn popper? If you don't use it, store it somewhere else where it won't be in the way, or give it away.
- Once dishes have been put away, you can hang the dish drainer on the wall until you need to use it again.

Create new counter space

- Fasten a hinged board to the wall that can be lowered when needed to create supplemental counter space in a jiffy.
- Turn your sink area into a temporary counter. Buy or cut a board wide enough to span the sink (making sure not to block the faucets) and you have a perfect area for washing and chopping vegetables.
- If you have enough floor space, consider purchasing a wheeled cart with a butcher-block top. They're incredibly versatile. Some carts, with drawers, shelves, and doors, can do double duty as an extra cabinet as well as work counter, while a lighter open-shelf model can double as a serving cart.

A word about comfort

• Is your counter too low? Raise it. A three-inch-thick cutting board will probably add enough height to straighten out your aching back.

Stepsavers

Pacing the floor

• Wearing out the floor (and yourself) traveling from range to work area to refrigerator? Keep a set of light appliances like toaster oven and electric frying pan near the sink, and make fast work of lunches, light meals, and snacks.
• A small wheeled cart is also handy for moving pots and crockery from one part of the range-sink-refrigerator work triangle to another.

Serving and clearing

• Store everyday dishes and silver close to the *eating* area, not the kitchen area, for easy table setting. Again, a mobile cart is handy for transferring dishes between kitchen and dining table. It's useful for transporting outdoor meals too.
• Consider creating a counter between kitchen and dining area, making a "window" for passing food and dishes back and forth. Your new counter can do triple duty as snack bar, storage space, and work area, while allowing you to chat with guests and family as you cook. You might find that construction costs are offset by the space-making benefits.

The Fine Art of Stashing and Storing

There are four cardinal principles of kitchen storage:

1. Access. Keep things you use most often most accessible. Stash rarely used items in your highest or deepest cabinets.

Laying hands on your Saturday night spaghetti pot shouldn't require pushing your way past the once-a-year Thanksgiving roaster.

2. Point of use. Wondering where to put something? Ask yourself: "Where do I usually stand when I use this utensil?" Keep the item close to the spot you've pinpointed; my cousin Marnie, for example, keeps her mug tree right next to the coffee pot.

3. Creative clustering. Cluster frequently used items together. Dinah, a serious baker, keeps her baking tins and gear, *and* flour, baking powder, and sugar in the same cabinet.

4. Dispersal. Not every saucepan has to be kept in the kitchen. Warehouse items used only for special occasions, or extras, in overflow storage spaces elsewhere in your home. Remember to list what you stash and where, and put the list in your "Household" file.

Get more mileage from your cabinets

- Transform a high shelf into two. Divide the shelf by slipping a freestanding wire shelf rack into the space.
- Hang cups, mugs, and small gadgets from hooks installed on the underside of shelves.
- Wasted space under your kitchen sink? Create new shelving with plastic storage bins or freestanding drawers on runners.

Two nifty ways to create new space

Double your kitchen storage space by hanging pots, pans, colanders, and kitchen tools.

- Line walls with precut grids or pegboard for hanging light items.
- Install a cast-iron or steel ceiling fixture to hang pots and pans.

Shelve it!

Create new shelf space where none existed before.

- Consider hanging your broom, dustpan, and mop outside the broom closet, and turn the closet into extra storage space by installing shelves. Consider using adjustable shelving, and if the space is deep, install pullout shelves, or store less frequently used things in the back.
- Check your wall for indentations of five inches or deeper. This space, shelved, is perfect for canned goods, spices, etc. If you like, add a door, and you've got a new cabinet.

Organize with organizers

Organizers are available for a host of uses, including lid covers, knives, food wraps and bags, cleaning products, and more. Many people believe—or hope—that store-bought organizers will organize them, but even the most clever device will become just another clutter opportunity if its use hasn't been thought through.

However, once you've thought about which organizers will work in your home, they can offer great storage alternatives. For example:

- Solve the problem of soft pouches (beans, grains, dried soups) by "filing" them in a narrow, box-type organizer.
- Wineglasses and other stemware can be hung from a rack that attaches under a cabinet.
- Purchase bins to organize cleaning supplies by task. Time to clean the oven? Just reach for the "oven cleaning" bin, and you're ready to go.

Improvise your own organizers

- A freestanding wine rack can also serve as a holder for rolled-up towels or napkins.
- Those six-pack cartons from beer or wine coolers are just the right size for storing baby's bottles.

Create your own pantry

In the good old days, most homes came equipped with large pantries, with enough space to store a year's worth of canned and dried goods. Today, few of us have even seen a pantry, much less enjoyed its benefits. But improvising on the old-fashioned pantry concept offers some real modern-day benefits, including fewer trips to the supermarket and having room to load up on specials.

Here are three ways to create space for bulk storage:

1. Use freestanding stackable plastic cubes for dried goods.
2. Tuck items into attractive covered floor baskets. One basket could hold a year's supply of soap bars.
3. Identify long-term storage opportunities for nonperishables elsewhere in your home. For example, a wicker trunk makes both a handsome coffee table and a handy storage unit.

Organizing the refrigerator

Your refrigerator is a "cold cabinet," to be organized like any other. Here are some tips.

- Keep frequently used items easily reachable and, where possible, group similar foods, such as cheeses, luncheon meats, etc. together.
- Choose a specific corner for leftovers that will keep them prominently visible, and check it every day. That way, you won't forget about that wonderful meat loaf, which is bound to grow a beard within a few days.
- Increase the mileage you get from the high main compartment by dividing the space not filled with bottles with "shelf-maker" organizers.

Freezer tips

- Put newer items in the back, and move older foods toward the front.

- Pick up some colored freezer labels and a permanent marker at the stationery store. Label each package appropriately, using the red labels for meat, yellow for poultry, green for vegetables, and be sure to note the date.

Buying a new refrigerator? Look for . . .

- Pull-out or revolving shelves so you can easily reach the items in the back.
- Adjustable shelves.
- Produce bins on the top, with the freezer located on the bottom or to the side. This keeps vegetables dry and easily accessible.

Add spices to your life

When it comes to organizing spices, pick what works for you.

- Alphabetize your spices, from anise to thyme. It really works to ensure quick and easy retrieval. *Or . . .*
- Keep "like" seasonings together. One dessert-making homemaker keeps the cinnamon, nutmeg, vanilla, and sprinkles on one caddy, and her general spices—basil, etc. —on another.

When it comes to storing spices:

- Insert a two-tiered lazy Susan in the kitchen cabinet, and keep tall containers toward the center, smaller ones on the outside. This method works best if you group "like" seasonings together. *Or . . .*
- Create an easy-access holder. Keep often-used spices close by in a countertop or hung holder. A long, narrow basket— usually used for rolls—will work well. Label *tops* of jars for easy access.

More kitchen-smart tips and tricks

- Divide contents of "large economy-size" packages into smaller containers to maintain freshness and for easier manageability.

- Two uses? Two places. Store your main flour supply with other baking materials, and keep a small container of flour near the range for sauces, gravy, etc.
- Keep a plastic flowerpot or container near the sink for potato peels, bruised lettuce leaves, and other scrapings. It keeps your sink clear, and it's great for the compost heap!
- Save bucks on Baggies. To reuse plastic bags, wash, slip a small magnet in each, and hang on the refrigerator to dry.

Groceries, Meal Planning and Preparation, Recipes, and Kid-Wise Kitchen Tips

Grocery shopping and menu planning

- Make up menu cards and reduce meal planning to about ten or fifteen minutes. Here's how:

  1. Compile recipes for twenty to thirty easy-to-prepare main dishes, and the same number of side dishes and desserts.
  2. Put each recipe on a 5″ x 8″ card, noting any special ingredients that would require a stop at a specialty shop.
  3. File all the recipe cards in a card box.
  4. Each week, select your required number of main-dish cards, mix and match them with side dishes and desserts, and your menu is complete. (Consider letting the kids pick the week's menus—meal planning can become a fun family project.)

- Patronize a market where your grocery order can be phoned in for later pickup or delivery.
- Design a "supermarket travel guide": Create a form with headings for each category—produce, meats and poultry, canned goods, etc. Leave spaces between each heading. Organize the form according to the layout of your supermarket (i.e., if the dairy case is the first place you go, then dairy should be your first heading).

Photocopy a quantity of these forms and store them in the kitchen. Enter items in the right categories as soon as you notice you're running low. Complete the list when you plan your weekly menus.

- Streamline unpacking at home by unloading your goods onto the checkout counter as they are arranged in your home, and ask the checker to pack the items as you have arranged them—refrigerator items together, canned goods together, etc. You'll be surprised to see how much this simplifies unpacking and putting things away.

- For you coupon users, here's a nifty tip from *Family Circle:* Write your shopping list on the back of an envelope, and stuff the envelope with the appropriate coupons.

A Minute Saved Is a Minute Earned

Some great timesavers require a little preparation time, so we often say, "I don't have enough time to do that." One way to appreciate the value of a good timesaver is to calculate the minutes saved using the tip. Here's how it works.

Preparation time. Note how much time it takes to prepare, say, the supermarket travel guide form. In this instance, it may take one and a half hours.

Estimate time saved. Using the supermarket form, time saved at home and in the supermarket per major visit is approximately twenty minutes.

Figure trips to supermarket needed to "earn out" the one and a half hours. Five trips earns the preparation time.

Payoff. After the fifth trip, the rest is gravy! Consider treating yourself to one of the "wishes" you've recorded on your Master List as a little reward.

Five ideas for streamlining cooking, baking, and meal preparation

1. Cook double, triple, and more! Then store one meal per bag in freezer bags that can be boiled or microwaved. Heat and eat.
2. No time to fuss with veggies? Treat yourself to precut vegetables at the salad bar in your local market. Just be sure to ask about sulfites if someone in your family is sensitive.
3. Ever have the phone ring when you're elbow deep in dough? Place a plastic bag by the phone, and slip the bag over your hand before answering to keep the phone clean.
4. A short shortening tip: Need less than a cup of solid shortening? It's easier to measure by cold-water displacement. For one-third cup of shortening, put two-thirds cup of cold water in your one-cup measure. Add shortening until the water level reaches the top. Then pour off the water.
5. Freeze small leftover portions in individual containers so you can pop them into the oven for a quick lunch or afternoon snack.

What to do with all those recipes

- Store recipes in magnetic photo albums according to category: soups, salads, baked goods, etc.
- Keep clipped recipes you've yet to try in an accordion-pleated envelope by category. When you're looking for something new, pull out a section that sounds good and go through it. That way, if Aunt Agatha's stew doesn't work for you, it's easy to toss and try Tom's goulash next time.
- Special diets? Keep a separate ring binder for low-fat and/or low-cholesterol recipes.
- To find cookbook favorites fast, write the names and page numbers on the inside cover of the cookbook.

Helping your children help out in the kitchen

Make kitchen chores family chores. Sharing makes easy work of meal preparation, table setting, and clearing. The trick to getting the kids involved is to make tasks doable for little fingers.

- Clip and paste magazine pictures of items stored in low cabinets—such as dishes, cereal boxes, etc.—to help your preschooler learn where things go.
- Keep the children's "kitchen stuff"—glasses, dishes, and even cereal boxes—within easy reach so they can help themselves as much as possible.
- For table setting, post a checklist of everything needed on the table for each meal on the inside door of a low cabinet. In addition to dishes and cutlery, don't forget salt and pepper shakers, filled water glasses, cut-up vegetables, etc.
- Baskets are easier (and safer) than trays for kids to use when clearing the table.
- Here's a nice idea from author Irvina Siegel Lew: Teach your toddler to set a table by coloring in shapes on a plain white paper place mat. Draw the shape of a fork, knife, spoon, plate, glass, and so on, and then give your little one plastic utensils to put in their proper places. Soon your child will want to set the table for everyone.

Fast and easy foods for baby

- Freeze baby food in the compartments of an ice-cube tray. Not only does this cut down on spoilage and waste, but it provides baby with an instant variety. Simply pop the cubes out, heat, and serve. (Two cubes generally make one three-ounce serving.)
- Cleanup is easy when you use an egg poacher to heat several different foods for baby at one time.

Get a grip on those milk spills

- Placing two rubber bands about an inch or so apart around a glass makes it easier for your toddler to grasp it.

Does your toddler love to toss everything out of your kitchen cabinet?

- Author Jean Gillies suggests inserting a yardstick vertically through a row of kitchen drawer handles to keep little fingers out of potential danger zones—like the utensil drawer.

16

Lightening the Load of Household Chores: Cleaning, Laundry, Errands, and More

The busywork of life—cleaning, laundry, and errands—can be made a little brisker and a little less tedious with the following techniques.

Tips for Hassle-Free Housecleaning

The more convenient your cleaning supplies, the faster the job

- Create mini–cleaning stations in strategic areas of your house—a plastic bin beneath your kitchen sink or next to the toilet in the bathroom is both practical and convenient.
- Keep bathtub cleaning supplies in a rack by the tub so each bather can swab after using.
- Keep a small hand vacuum near the living room for quick sweep-ups. I recommend having two floor vacuum cleaners: a light one for your weekly routine and a heavy-duty model for major monthly cleanups.
- Smudgy mirror? Glass tabletop? Keep a small bottle of glass cleaner and a cloth in a nearby drawer.

Getting at those hard-to-reach places

• Dust and dirt under a refrigerator can interfere with the cooling system. To reach that grungy place, attach an old sock to the end of a yardstick or broom handle with a rubber band. Slip the stick under the refrigerator and slide from side to side to clean the floor. The same technique works for brushing away cobwebs in hard-to-reach corners of the room.

Creative cleaning tools: did you know . . .

• A toy carpet sweeper is great for stair treads.
• A soft paintbrush is perfect for dusting lamp shades, picture frames, and louvered doors.

Household help

• You may find it's cost-effective to hire a half- or full-day-a-week cleaning person. Draw up a list of regular assignments for your helper. Make sure you define *your* priorities in order to make the best use of his or her time. Be sure to discuss cleaning products—*you* know your antique wooden desk requires special treatment, but she won't unless you tell her.
• You may opt for a professional cleaning service—a team of people who come on a contract basis and clean the whole house in a few hours. Cleaning services can also be hired "as needed" for heavy-duty jobs like cleaning out the basement. Check the Yellow Pages under "Cleaning Services" or "House Cleaning." Be aware that many of these services, which tend to be more expensive than home helpers, will not do chores such as washing dishes.

A Few Laundry and Dry-Cleaning Tips

Simple sorting

- Do you have more than one child around the same age and size? Distinguish their clothes by marking a colored dot on the garment label where it won't be seen. Use a different color for each child.
- Cut down on sheet confusion by marking *each corner* of each sheet with a *T, F, Q,* or *K* (twin, full, queen, or king).
- Large family? Put a hamper in each person's room. Launder only one or two hampers at a time—it cuts down on sorting.

Sock solutions

- Buy socks by the dozen, since they get eaten up.
- Pin socks together in pairs. Give older children a set of diaper pins, each with their own color, to pin socks together before putting them in the hamper.

Laundry efficiency

- Start a load of laundry before you go to work. Bed linens can be stripped and washed in the morning, and dried when you get home.
- *Before washing:* Sort laundry according to washing instructions—warm water, cold water, bleach, etc.
  After washing: Sort items according to destination—all of Billy's clothes go into one basket, yours into another. *Or* . . .
- Designate an individual shelf or colorful plastic basket for each person in the family. When the laundry's done, stack the clean clothes on the appropriate shelves so they can pick them up and put them away.
- Special apartment-house tips: Try to do the wash in the off-hours. Save steps by stacking the "done" clothes in your laundry cart according to their route in your apartment. If the kitchen is near the front door, potholders and kitchen towels go on top of the pile, and so on.

Delicate garments

• To save the time and bother of hand washing, machine wash your delicate garments in a wide mesh bag.

To call a stain or repair to your dry cleaner's attention

• Mark your own stains. Ask your dry cleaner for a roll of stain stickers, or tear off a piece of the adhesive part of a yellow Post-it and put it on the stain. Before stickering a garment for the first time, make sure the fabric isn't affected by testing a sticker on an inner seam.

Living with Linens

Four ideas about storing your linens

1. Label linen closet shelves Twin, Full, Queen, and King.
2. Simplify by choosing characteristic colors or patterns for different-size sheets: all double-bed sheets might be white, all twin-bed yellow, and so on.
3. Create coordinated sets: Fold pillowcases and top sheet inside the bottom sheet, so you can quickly grab the set you're looking for.
4. Limited linen closet space? Store bed linens in a dresser or on a closet shelf in each bedroom. Or convert an armoire to serve as a linen closet.

Towel tips

• Roll 'em, don't fold 'em—and save space. Stack the rolls on top of each other, or side by side in rows.
• Short on towel racks? Put towel hooks on the wall.
• If you have too many towels for your linen closet, why not keep them in the bathroom? A wicker three-shelf rack on your bathroom wall makes an attractive display area for folded towels.

- Put the freshly laundered towels at the bottom of your towel pile to avoid mildew and mustiness.

. . . and tablecloths

- If you're short on space, try hanging tablecloths on sturdy hangers or on towel racks mounted on the back of the linen closet door.

Shopping, Errands, and Chores: A Roundup of Tips

Some of the following tips have been mentioned elsewhere in this book, but they bear repeating as they are key to making quick work of tedious, time-consuming jobs.

Consolidate errands and small jobs

- Do all your errands in one location at a time. While you're out, check your errands list to see if you can knock off any other things-to-do in the same neighborhood.

Let someone else do it

- Hire a student to be an errand runner and to take care of basic pickups and deliveries. Hire students for other chores around the house, such as cleaning out the garage.
- Barter. You hate to scrub floors? Your sister hates to do her bills? Swap services.
- Negotiate with your spouse—his/her most hated for your most hated. Make sure you negotiate equitably—you'll do the grocery shopping if he washes and tunes up your car.

Smart shopping

- Shopping doesn't have to be mom's job. Train your family to be smart shoppers, and let them share the load. Kids are often happy to shop for their own clothes and school supplies—and they can shop for food as well. Spouses unused to grocery shopping can be trained with a list, a budget, and gentle instructions.

- Buy in bulk and save. Many items like beer and soft drinks, health and beauty aids, and bathroom supplies can be purchased through discount distributors at much lower than retail prices. Inquire as to delivery or carry-out-to-your-car services.
- Shop by mail. Cut down on trips to the store by taking advantage of catalogs. This could also take some of the stress out of the holiday season.

Kiddie shopping

- Do you have growing kids at home? Always keep a list of current sizes with you and pick up bargains when you see them. This way you'll never bring home the wrong size. Remeasure every month or so.

17

Family Organizing—
How to Make It Work

Getting Everyone Involved

Whether you're a single parent with one child or a blended family with five children, your household will run more smoothly if you involve your children in the organizational process. Not only will you enjoy the help of some extra hands, but by giving your children some familial responsibility you are exposing them to the healthy dynamic of teamwork and allowing them the pride and satisfaction of contributing to the family's well-being.

Trouble begins, however, when tasks (1) are not clearly defined; (2) are inappropriate for a child's age; or (3) become a power struggle between parent and child.

The key to organizing your family effectively is to create definite jobs with clear-cut responsibilities for your children. When a child is assigned a specific job appropriate to his or her age and skills, he or she is usually proud to take part in the family's decision-making process.

The following techniques have proven effective in many families:

The five-step "brownie point" method

1. Have the family agree on a point value for each task—taking out the garbage, five points; sweeping the driveway, ten points, etc. Base your point system on how long the task takes and how difficult it is. Remember that children's tasks should be weighted according to their ages and skills.
2. Each person contracts for a fixed number of points each week, based on his or her ability and fixed time constraints.
3. Cut chips out of construction paper. Write the job description on one side of the chip and its point value on the other. (Write "little people" jobs on different-colored chips.)
4. "Go fish" for jobs. Each family member draws a chip, point side up, and then turns the chip over to find out what the job is. All members should keep drawing until the pre-agreed number of points has been reached.
5. Make a master list of the tasks, including the time of day when they are to be completed—before school, immediately after school, by dinner time, etc.—and post it on the refrigerator.

Share family responsibilities

- Institute an "adopt-a-meal" program. Each "eligible" family member is responsible for one or two meals a week, from menu planning, shopping, and preparing the food to setting the table and cleaning up. Allow the young chefs to add their shopping list to mom's.
- Alternate jobs each week to combat boredom, and remember to acknowledge good work. To keep track of who does which chores when, use an erasable marker and plastic wall calendar.
- Put one of the older children in charge of setting the breakfast table the night before.
- Youngsters make wonderful picker-uppers. Ask your child to pick up toys and clutter left around the house and collect them in an old pillowcase. (It's best not to use plastic bags around small children.)
- Schedule a weekly family workday for major projects.

Personal "must-do" chores

- Apart from general family chores, each person in the household should be responsible for:

  1. Hanging/folding their own clothes, and putting personal belongings away at night, especially clutter-conducive items like books, toys, and computer gear
  2. Making their bed each morning
  3. Putting laundry into the proper basket in the laundry room

Divest spouse chores of the power struggle

- Division of labor between spouses is often a major bone of contention. She says *he* always leaves his clothes strewn around the room. He says *she* always sends the bills out late.

  The solution is to negotiate. Hammer out deals. Draw up a list of chores and determine which tasks each of you prefers doing. Maybe you don't mind picking up after him, if he washes and services your car. As you work through dividing tasks, make sure you come up with an equitable deal.

The family telegraph

A major component in achieving familial organization—as well as in keeping the peace—is clear communication. To avoid mixed signals, try these ideas.

- Turn a bulletin board into a family communication center. Keep a running list of grocery items that need replacing, important telephone numbers—mom and dad at work, doctor, police, etc.—and family reminders. Also post a list of instructions: what to do in case of fire, if the baby-sitter doesn't show up, etc.
- Posting "Went to the store, be back in 5," on the fridge is a great way to communicate with family members. Keep a

filled Post-its holder on the wall with a pen or marker to save you from scrambling through drawers in search of scrap paper.

- Keep a pad of "While you were out" message slips by each phone.
- Keep a household loose-leaf binder of general information: phone numbers of your kids' friends, neighbors, repair people; train timetables and your bus schedules; takeout menus. This is also a handy place to keep coupons.

Your Kids *Can* Get Organized!

Your kids are capable of getting organized—and enjoying it— despite what you might think. Young children do prefer living in an orderly way, but they often lose interest in organization when it turns into a power struggle. Many children learn to ignore such orders as "Clean up your room!" and "Put your toys away *now!*" very early on.

What's the solution? *Start early.* Believe it or not, you can begin instilling good organizing attitudes as soon as your child is capable of sorting blocks into one pile and crayons into another.

Start with these three helpful principles.

1. In planning your child's room, bear in mind his/her preferences and capabilities. Set up a room which he or she can easily manage.
2. Remember that the ability to organize is a *learned skill*— like learning to read. Reward orderliness with praise, as you would any other achievement.
3. Match the chore to the child. Assign tasks realistically to minimize frustration and increase the child's sense of accomplishment and mastery.

Organizing Your Kids' Clothes and Closets

Fit the closet to the child

- Ask the store to give you the hanger that comes with the child's garment. It's a money saver, and it's frequently hard to find little hangers that fit little clothes.
- Line the closet door with a few stick-on hooks at the child's eye level so he can hang his own pajamas and robes.
- When the child can negotiate hangers, insert a tension rod in the closet. Adjust the height as she grows.

Dirty clothes

- Put a small hamper in the bedroom (not the bathroom) so the kids can drop in their dirty clothes "as they go." Make a game of it for very young children, and they'll get in the habit early.

Color-coding for your kids

- Try color-coding your children's things to make them easily identifiable and foster self-reliance. Perhaps Michael is blue —blue towels, blue toothbrush, and blue sheets—while Melissa is yellow. Let them choose their own color.
- Paint clothes drawers different colors for different clothes: T-shirts, sweaters, underwear . . . or use colored stickers.
- Stackable colored plastic cubes make great storage bins for extra T-shirts, toys, puzzles, and games. Stacked, they make nifty room dividers if two kids share one room.

The Toy Wars

The toy chest is the perfect example of an organizing technique that should work, but doesn't. A toy chest provides plenty of bulk storage, but finding a particular toy in it is next to impossible. Invariably, your little one winds up flinging countless toys on the floor to get to his favorite whistle, as you watch in helpless frustration.

Your Child-Scaling Checklist

☐   Is your kids' furniture hazardproof and durable? Look for easy-care materials, round edges, and simple designs that won't catch excessive dust and grit.

☐   Can your child see over the top of the dresser?

☐   Are drawers easy to maneuver? Check that knobs are well formed so your child can get a firm grip.

The key to organization for a small child is, surprisingly enough, precise placement. Most children are happy to give each toy or game its own home. Here's how to do it:

First, install shelves

• Line the walls of your child's room with low shelves to spread out cars and trucks, puzzles, dolls, stuffed toys, books, games, robots, and everything else. Use adjustable shelves that can be raised as the child grows.

Second, organize your child's shelf space

• Give each plaything its own space on the shelf. Fill shelves with bright-colored plastic trays or containers, making sure to match size to contents: small boxes for marbles, medium for crayons, etc. Children learn quickly that "the little cars go on the medium blue tray," "the pick-up sticks go on the thin green tray." *Or . . .*

• Affix brightly colored stickers to plain containers, or simply paint the shelves. The color-code connection works the same.

Need additional shelf space?

Here are a few alternatives, depending on your space configurations.

- If there is extra space in the room, try freestanding wire shelves.
- If there's extra space in a closet, convert that space into shelf space by inserting a freestanding shelf rack.
- Shelve the space between two indents in a wall.

For play-in-progress

- With your child, choose a corner of the room for play-in-progress. This is where he can lay out that jigsaw puzzle or Lego city.

Toy overload?

- Every six months you and your child should pack up those toys she has lost interest in, store them for six months, then sort through them again. Keep those toys that have regained their freshness, and discard the rest.
- Many kids (like many adults) are pack rats—they don't want it, they don't use it, they don't even like it—but they won't give it up. When your child has trouble letting go, encourage her to donate unused toys to a local hospital or children's home. Many children get genuine pleasure from feeling that their belongings are going to a new home with children who will value them.

Getting Your Small Child Off to a Good Organizing Start

Many parents are surprised to find that even tiny tots are capable of learning and practicing good organizing skills. The key is to engage them creatively—and they will learn early that organizing can be fun.

Create organizing games

Start with a general recognition exercise, then advance to the more specific skills of sorting and matching.

- Put some shoes around the room, and ask your child to find them, and bring them to "the shoe place"—a designated corner.
- Can your child stack up all the blocks in one place and all the crayons in another? Reward with a kiss and a star.
- Ask your little one to put together the socks that are alike.
- Here's a neat way to teach more sophisticated category conceptualization: My friend Muriel, whose son Oliver was stumped by an Alice-in-Wonderland puzzle, asked him to first find all the white pieces that formed Alice's apron. Then she asked him to collect all the straight-edged border pieces, and so forth. By breaking down the puzzle this way, Oliver not only mastered it, but in the process sharpened his concentration skills.

The three-step clean-your-own-room plan

Step 1. Make a chart for your child's bedroom door with columns across the top listing the tasks you and the child have agreed he/she will do—"Make bed," "Put away toys," "Pick up clothes." Write the days of the week down the side. If the child can't read yet, choose appropriate pictures from magazines together and paste them with the appropriate headings.

Step 2. Agree to an inspection time, when tasks are supposed to be completed. (At other times, ignore the mess.)

Step 3. At inspection time, put a gold star on the chart for each task accomplished. The Kellys had a "keeper-of-her-room" celebration, complete with diploma, when their daughter Bonnie had successfully mastered all her tasks for two consecutive months.

Child-scale tasks

Arrange your home to foster your child's self-reliance. Quite a few tasks can be made doable for small children. For example:

- A four-year-old can get her own glass of milk if it's pre-poured into a plastic cup in the fridge.
- Buy clothing with simple catches and fastenings, so your child can learn to dress himself as early as possible. Get sneakers with Velcro tabs, flat tube socks without heels.
- Use a comforter so the child can make the bed up easily.

Kiddie logistics

- Pool child-care resources: Carpools, baby-sitting pools, co-ops, and play groups are great ways of saving time and getting the kids to and fro.
- Save time by creating a form letter for routine correspondence with your child's school—excuses from class (for rehearsal, medical appointment, other), and permission to engage in activities.
- To keep track of family activities, get a monthly hanging calendar with the biggest date squares you can find. At the beginning of each month, write in regular appointments—ballet lessons, Cub Scout meetings, carpooling arrangements. Use a different color marker for each child. Fill in special events, like birthday parties, as well. As a backup, note these dates in your personal calendar too.

18

Rooms and Other Spaces— Adding Comfort to Your Home

Living comfortably in your home is as much a function of organization as of eliminating clutter. Being able to move around comfortably, having at hand what you need, and having sufficient space for convenient living can vastly improve the quality of your life. This chapter is devoted to helping you increase your comfort and efficiency at home.

The Family Room

Because the family room is often the hub of so many different activities—entertaining, playing with the kids, talking, snacking, reading, or watching TV—it often becomes an organizational trouble spot in many homes. Here are four ways to keep your family happy in the family room:

1. Food and drinks everywhere? Place end tables at every chair and couch for snacks and drinks. Buy small Masonite tables and cover them with cloths, or if you don't have space for permanent end tables, look for "occasional" tables with wheels that can be easily moved.
2. Preventing spills or stains: Protect furniture with vinyls, glazed chintzes, or other waterproof or stain-resistant fabric. Some families protect their furniture with inexpensive

throws, which can be attached by sewing on snaps and easily removed for company.

3. Create a children's corner: stock the area with toys, games, drawing paper, and pens on shelves or in a low cabinet.

4. Does the family room double as your exercise studio? Buy a tall cylindrical basket in which to store a rolled-up exercise mat. Store weights and other small equipment, like sweatbands or a stopwatch, in a decorative box or chest, and hang your exercise togs and jump rope on hooks in a nearby closet.

The Bedroom

Many of us snack in bed, read, talk on the phone, play card games, watch television, sew, or knit. Here are some ideas for creating a comfortable and convenient bedside area.

Bedside boosters

- Many of the things you need—a nail care kit, note paper, playing cards—will fit into the drawer of your nighttable. A basket under the bed or hung from a wall hook is a handy place for a mending or knitting satchel.

- For easy access to writing supplies, tissues, or your favorite book, create a simple, no-frills bed caddy from a sturdy pocket of cloth which is secured to the bed by slipping a long flap of the material between the mattress and box spring. It's even simpler to toss these things into a straw bedside basket.

Get comfortable

Almost everybody reads or watches TV in bed, but virtually nobody is really organized for it.

- Prop yourself up to read with a bolster. Some bolsters have pockets for pencils, paperbacks, etc.

- A late-night reader whose spouse goes to sleep earlier can switch from a regular reading lamp to a small, high-intensity lamp that clips to the book and illuminates only the page.
- For you "late show" watchers, improve your marriage by buying a headset attachment for your TV, and let your spouse sleep in peace.

Practical beds

- Consider a platform bed fitted with big drawers to store extra bedding or off-season clothes.
- Consider creative headboards. Purchase a ready-made or custom-made headboard that provides you with extra storage capacity. A headboard unit with a false top that lifts can double as a cabinet and/or bookshelf.

The Bathroom

Organizing the medicine cabinet

- Your medicine cabinet is a little closet. For easy access, organize it logically by type of product: store the products you use daily, like toothpaste or floss, where they are easily accessible; store items you seldom use, like NyQuil or suntan lotion, on a higher shelf or in the back.
- Every three months or so, check through the cabinet and throw out the products you've stopped using, particularly cosmetics, which can actually "spoil."
- Note the purchase date on all over-the-counter medications and toss a year after opening.
- Post first-aid instructions on the inside door of the cabinet "just in case," and always keep a first-aid kit—complete with bandages and antiseptic—well within reach. (P.S. Keep another first-aid kit in the kitchen, which is where you're most apt to suffer a cut or burn.)

What to do with prescription drugs

- Ironically, most medicine cabinets are too humid to properly store medicines. Keep medication in a dry, cool, dark closet or pantry, preferably on a high shelf, especially if you have small children. One family packed potentially dangerous medications into a locked box which they kept in the parents' bedroom.
- To manage many medications, buy a pillbox with seven sections and fill it once a week.

Bathe and shower in comfort

- When you shower, do you have to fight your way through a battalion of shampoo bottles, conditioners, and "one-minute miracle" hair treatments? Consolidate! Put all this stuff either in a hanging tiered wire basket, or in a caddy that hangs over the shower nozzle. There are also shower curtains with pockets for shampoo and soap. Choose the organizer appropriate for the design of your individual shower.

Three no-fail tips to keep cosmetics and toiletries handy

1. Keep curling irons and blow-dryers in a basket on top of the toilet or under the sink, or hang them from nails or hooks on the walls. Of course, always be sure to keep electrical items far away from a water source.
2. Use baskets and other containers to hold your everyday makeup. My cousin the makeup fanatic sorts her big stash by category—eyeliners, blush, eye shadow—for easy retrieval. She then stands the elongated items, like mascara, eye pencils, makeup brushes, and cotton swabs, upright in plastic cups.
3. Clear kitchen canisters work well for cotton balls, Q-tips, cotton pads, small makeup sponges, and the like.

Bathroom supplies made simple

- Keep bathroom supplies—tissues, toilet paper, stocks of soaps—in or near the bathroom, rather than in a linen closet. If that's not possible . . .
- Keep at least one spare roll of toilet tissue and tissues in each bathroom. Store backup bulky items in a linen closet, or on a clothes closet shelf. I recommend storing cleaning supplies, which have strong chemicals, separately from towels, sheets, or clothing—perhaps under the bathroom sink.
- If you have a pedestal sink, create ad hoc storage by lining the sink with a skirt. Insert Rubbermaid "instant shelves," preferably pull-out, or a slide-out two-tiered wire basket. For less frequently used articles, store a turntable in the back.

Tight hamper space?

- Fit a hamper or perhaps a small recycling bin in the space between your sink and toilet, or toilet and tub. Or, if you aren't utilizing the skirted space under your pedestal sink, store a small clothes hamper there.

Three more bathroom convenience tips

1. Install a paper-cup dispenser. It's convenient and sanitary—and there'll be fewer glasses for you to wash.
2. Also install a paper towel dispenser and make quick work of fast cleanup jobs.
3. Place a sponge on a soap dish (with holes) right above the sink. Encourage family members to wipe the sink after each use.

See pages 174–175 for helpful hints on towels and linens.

The Workroom—Sewing, Knitting, and Crafts

Arts and crafts projects often entail working with materials of various sizes and shapes, and your enjoyment can turn to frustration if you try to work in a confusing and cluttered work area. The following hints will help you unclutter your arts and crafts supplies.

Seven tips for storing and handling sewing supplies

1. An empty thermometer case is a handy holder for extra-long needles. Mary Ellen suggests keeping a small magnet in your sewing basket to attract pins and needles that drop during sewing.
2. Notions—cards of snaps, seam binding, rickrack, zippers, etc.—should be stored upright in a small box, or thumbtacked to a bulletin board or corkboard.
3. Keep buttons, sorted by size and color, in small zip-top plastic bags. Extra-small buttons fit nicely into snap-top plastic pill containers.
4. Store fabrics and projects in clear plastic boxes on open shelves or in a trunk. The bottom part of the trunk is perfect for laying out fabric, and if there's a tray on top, it can be used to hold patterns.
5. Mark patterns for future projects by pinning a small swatch of the fabric you plan to use onto the envelope. Store patterns you are not currently using in an expanding file.
6. To keep track of several ongoing projects, list each one you're working on, your deadline, if any, and what stage it's in. Pin the list to the wall or bulletin board and update it each time you work. Apply the same principle to artwork or handiwork projects.
7. Convenient access to tools is an important part of needlework. Get into working position and "walk through" the motions of each process. Place the most frequently used supplies near where your hand rests most comfortably.

Hang your scissors on a wall hook most convenient to where you cut out patterns.

Knitting boosters

- Hang your skeins from low hooks on the wall near your favorite chair.
- To keep your yarn straight when you're working with more than one ball, put all the balls in a plastic bag. Then punch out small holes. Thread the end of each yarn through a separate hole and they won't tangle.

Storing craft materials

- Use plastic cutlery trays to store paints, glue, beads, paint brushes, and other craft materials.
- Fill empty nail polish bottles with paint, lacquer, etc. and keep handy for small touch-ups.

Workroom and handiwork

- Need to come up with a system for easy tool retrieval? Think pegboard. Once you've hung the tools, outlining each one gives you foolproof guidelines for easy cleanup.
- For tools that aren't hangable, consider a bin on wheels, which you keep under your work counter when not in use.
- Color-code shelving for each category in your workroom, so you'll always know exactly where painting supplies, gardening supplies, and bicycle gear go.
- Fill a few small jars with the most frequently used nails and screws. Arrange them out of the way on your work counter, or nail the tops of the jars to the underside of a convenient shelf. Then screw each corresponding jar into its top.
- Here's an idea for getting repeat uses out of a paint roller pan: Before beginning a paint job, put a large plastic bag over the pan. *Then* pour the paint in. When the job is finished, pull off and toss the plastic bag.

Some Ingenious Solutions for Small Spaces

In today's world, living space is often at a premium, and figuring out how to live comfortably in a limited space can be very challenging. Here's how to make the most of a studio apartment, a miniloft, or any small area in your home that you feel is underutilized.

The key is to divide and conquer. Look for ways to separate spaces and maximize the use of small areas. In many cases you can accomplish wonders with little or no construction.

Four suggestions for taking advantage of existing features

- Turn an alcove into a small "reading room" or breakfast nook.
- Convert a walk-in closet into a mini-office.
- Make wide corridors functional. One writer converted part of her wide hallway into a small office by setting up a space-efficient desk (with filing space underneath) flush against the wall.
- Doors can always be removed, or rehinged to swing in the opposite direction. This technique may come in handy in rethinking your space.

Create new spaces

- "Conceal and disguise" to divide living, work, and leisure spaces. Hide a mini-office in your bedroom with a folding screen. The bedroom side of the screen is also a neat place to display scarves and jewelry from nails or hooks.

More about partitions

To create separate rooms . . .

- Ceiling-to-floor roller blinds, cut to size, can make two rooms out of one—or partition off any special corner, such as a Sunday painter's "studio."

- A bank of stacked storage cubes or high bookcases will also create special rooms. This tip also creates storage space for books, CDs, sweaters, plants, and more.

To divide rooms . . .

- Light, mobile partitions and screens are your simplest solution. You can create your own by covering burlap screens with fabric or marbleized paper. Put the screens on casters for greater mobility.
- A row or cluster of large plants and small trees is an attractive method for defining separate areas.
- A serving counter between the kitchen and dining area provides a unique space-saving opportunity. It not only helps define the space, but also cuts down on your back-and-forth time.

Divide vertical space too

- High ceilings? Build a loft, and you've got a new room. A 7′ × 9′ loft is good for a small office; if you can squeeze out an 8′ × 10′ loft, you've got an extra bedroom. Idea: Attach roller blinds to hide the below-loft space and use it for storage. (Be advised that building a loft will take significant construction.)

Back-to-back your way into saving space

Your living room should have an open area of at least five feet square to give you room to move around in. To achieve this, cluster your furniture so that it touches or is linked.

- Back a couch with a dining table or desk.
- Create two "living areas" by placing two couches back-to-back.
- Improvise a headboard for your bed by backing it with a sturdy chest of drawers, the back of a stacked-cube storage arrangement, or the back of a bookcase.

Make your furniture do double duty

Using furniture as storage units is another great way to make the most of your limited space.

- A large covered basket containing clothes, linens, or dry or canned food can double as an occasional table or ottoman —just cover it with cushions. You can also cluster baskets (in which you store things) in a corner with plants.
- A two-drawer lateral filing cabinet makes a nifty coffee table. Top it off with a laminated butcher block cut to size. Just be sure to store heavy materials in the bottom drawer to keep your "coffee table" steady. Trunks can also double as coffee tables.
- Turn a sturdy wicker chest into a coffee table, end table, or, covered with cushions, a window seat.
- If you have a table with a lower shelf, cover the table with a cloth and use the shelf to store extra blankets, pillows, etc.

Efficiency sleeping arrangements

- The most convenient sleeping alternative is still the traditional convertible couch. There are also some chairs on the market that open up into beds, and the futon has emerged as a doable bed/sofa combination. Your choice simply depends on your individual preference and how much space you have.
- The daybed, a single bed covered with a throw and some pillows, doubles as a couch during the day and a bed at night. Some daybeds are fitted with a "trundle bed" underneath that slides out to expand into a double bed.
- Before buying any piece that expands, opens, or otherwise changes position, be sure to measure the space it will occupy when open. A friend of mine thought she was being clever when she purchased a Murphy bed. Unfortunately, she failed to measure the space between the open bed and the bathroom door. The good news is she can literally roll out of bed and land in the bathroom. The bad news is she has to squeeze through an eight-inch opening to do so.

The Organized Auto

The smallest "room" you spend any time in is probably your car. Spending a few minutes to make it an efficient, comfortable space is a worthwhile investment.

While driving

- Put a language tape in your tape deck, and freshen up your French.
- Here's a nice way to get some reading done while on the road: Do you and your spouse both like to read the newspaper and some of the same magazines? Use driving time together as a chance for the non-driver to read out loud for both of you.

While you're waiting

We spend lots of time on the road and our minutes count. So why not turn some of that lost time—waiting for the kids, stuck in traffic—into found time?

- Keep a file of "quickie" paper tasks, such as magazine subscriptions to send in, school notes to review, etc., in the glove compartment to take care of while you're waiting for the kids to come out of band practice. Or use the time to flip through a catalog or two.
- Even more ambitious: Use your car as a mini-office where you can update your expense accounts, write notes to clients, and review your to-do list. You'll need a "traveling work kit" in the glove compartment, which should include notepaper, envelopes, Post-its, stamps, pen, highlighter, calculator, and 3" x 5" cards to jot notes on. This can be very useful if you are waiting for an oil change, tire rotation, or the like.
- Stopped in traffic? Touch up makeup or nails with a small kit kept in the glove compartment. Don't forget to keep your eyes on the road.

- Do a quick car cleaning. Collect the toys, cassette tapes, and articles of clothing from the floor and pile them in a giant shopping bag. (Keep a supply of bags in the trunk.) Use a lint remover to pick up pet hairs and cookie crumbs.
- Try a quick de-stressor. Close your eyes, take a few slow, deep breaths, and imagine each part of your body relaxing —starting with feet and ankles and working your way up to the top of your head.
- Brief chunks of waiting time are great for focusing your attention on minor dilemmas. Think about ways to re-arrange the den to accommodate the new computer, how to keep the cat from waking you at 5:00 A.M.; how you and a colleague will split responsibilities when she comes back from maternity leave.
- Planning a driving vacation? Scan maps of the area and plot your route.
- Enjoy a few precious minutes of not doing a thing!

Keeping track of mileage and other record-keeping chores

- Keep receipts for new tires, oil changes, and repair work in an envelope in the glove compartment. Jot down the next date for an oil change, tune-up, and tire rotation on the outside of the envelope and enter those dates in your calendar. You might get a higher price when you sell your car or trade it in if you can show you've been servicing it faithfully.
- Keep a mileage notebook in your glove compartment to record gasoline expenses and miles driven for business, charity, and medical purposes. These miles are partially tax-deductible. Some of your car maintenance expenses might also be deductible, so keep those receipts!

Getting from here to there—maps and directions

- Tired of hearing your friends say, "You need directions *again?* You've been here a million times!"? Keep a file of directions to places you expect to return to. You'll save time

and effort when you don't have to call and take down the
same directions again and again.
- Keep often-used maps in your visor, side pocket, the glove
compartment, or anywhere they're easily accessible to you
in the driver's seat. For longer trips, organize maps in the
order in which you will need them. Some drivers attach
maps to their visor with a rubber band or clip.

Traveling with kids

- The secret of happy car travel with kids is to keep them
occupied. Stock the car with loads of activity books, crossword puzzles, little games such as "drop the silver balls in
the hole," books, etc. Store all the goodies in a car organizer
that hangs down the back of the front seat, or improvise
your own organizer by stashing the gear in a lingerie bag
with pockets.
- Keep a work pouch in the car filled with markers, crayons,
pencils, drawing paper, stickers, stars, etc.
- Check some children's story tapes out of the library and
play them on the car tape deck.

Trunk tips

- Put together a cold-weather kit, which should include de-
icing spray, a windshield scraper, jumper cables, some clean
rags, antifreeze, and a small bag of rock salt. Keep a bag of
sand or kitty litter to provide extra traction on ice.
- Wrap safety tools and flares together in a blanket to prevent
them from rolling around. The blanket will also prove useful should you ever have to crawl under the car.

And for overall car convenience . . .

- Keep change for meters and tolls in a taxicab driver's coin
dispenser or portable coinholder.

- Store a folding umbrella in a side pocket or under the passenger seat where you can easily reach it in case of a sudden downpour.
- Hang a small plastic trash bag from an ashtray, stereo knob, or glove compartment handle for stray wrappers, gum, and lint that would otherwise end up on the floor.
- For a quick touch-up on your headlights and windows, stash a small spray bottle of window cleaner and paper towels in the car.
- Keep a pack of Post-its in the glove compartment. Write down reminders like, "Have oil checked," "Pick up milk on the way home," and put them on the dashboard. Peel them off and throw away when the errand is completed.

And here are two zippy tips attributed to Jeffrey Katzenberg, the legendarily efficient film executive:

- When he was at Paramount Pictures, Katzenberg timed the traffic lights so he could make the ordinarily 20-minute drive home in 9 minutes.
- He traded his Porsche for an automatic-shift Mustang so his hands would be free for the phone.

Send us *your* best tips!

Congratulations! You've done great work—and now please tell us about *your* organizing experience. In the never-ending quest to keep us all better organized, please send your best organizing and time management tips to:

Stephanie Winston
c/o Simon & Schuster
1230 Avenue of the Americas
New York, NY 10020

I will personally review every suggestion you send for a possible follow-up book.

. . . .

Here are organizing and time management tips I've found useful: _____

_____

_____

_____

_____

_____

_____

(Please feel free to attach additional sheets.)

If we were to write a sequel, what new topics should we include? _____

_____

_____

_____

_____

Any other comments? _____

_____

_____

_____

Thanks! Please photocopy or tear this sheet out.

Bibliography

Bracken, Peg. *I Hate to Housekeep Book.* New York: Harcourt, Brace & World, 1962. (Paperback: Fawcett Crest, 1965.)

Eisenberg, Ronni, with Kate Kelly. *Organize Yourself!* New York: Collier/Macmillan, 1986.

Faux, Marian. *Successful Free-lancing.* New York: St. Martin's Press, 1982.

Gillies, Jean. *How to Run Your House without Letting It Run You.* Garden City, N.Y.: Doubleday, 1973.

Hedrick, Lucy H. *Five Days to an Organized Life.* New York: Dell, 1990.

Lakein, Alan. *How to Get Control of Your Time and Your Life.* New York: New American Library, 1973, 1989.

Lew, Irvina Siegel. *You Can't Do It All: Ideas That Work for Mothers Who Work.* New York: Atheneum, 1986.

Mackenzie, Alec. *The Time Trap: The New Version of the 20-Year Classic on Time Management.* New York: AMACOM, 1990, 1991.

Mayer, Jeffrey J. *If You Haven't Got the Time to Do It Right, When Will You Find the Time to Do It Over?* New York: Simon & Schuster, 1990.

Pinkham, Mary Ellen. *Mary Ellen's Best of Helpful Hints.* New York: Warner Books, 1979.

Schlenger, Sunny, and Roesch, Roberta. *How to Be Organized in Spite of Yourself.* New York: New American Library, 1989.

Stoddard, Alexandra. *Style for Living: How to Make Where You Live You.* Garden City, N.Y.: Doubleday, 1974.

Townsend, Robert. *Up the Organization.* New York: Fawcett, 1970.

Winston, Stephanie. *Getting Organized: The Easy Way to Put Your Life in Order.* Rev. ed. New York: Warner Books, 1991.

———. *The Organized Executive: New Ways to Manage Time, Paper, People & the Electronic Office.* Rev. ed. New York: Warner Books, 1994.

Index